HAL LEONARD UKULELE CHORD FINDER

Easy-to-Use Guide to Over 1000 Ukulele Chords

by Chad Johnson

D1358306

ISBN 0-634-06864-4

In Australia Contact:
Hal Leonard Australia Pty. Ltd
22 Taunton Drive P.O. Box 5130
Cheltenham East, 3192 Victoria, Australia
Email: ausadmin@halleonard.com

Visit Hal Leonard Online at www.halleonard.com

HAL•LEONARD®
CORPORATION
7777 W. BLUEMOUND RD. P.O. BOX 13819 MILWAUKEE, WI 53213

TABLE OF CONTENTS

INTRODUCTION

Ukulele Chord Finder is an extensive reference guide to over 1,000 chords. Twenty-eight different chord qualities are covered for each key, and each chord quality is presented in three different voicings. Open strings are used when possible, but at least one voicing from each quality will be a moveable form. This allows for many unique voicings but also provides practical chord forms that can be transposed to any key. One thing to remember is that many of these moveable forms are also unique. So, just because you've learned two moveable shapes for C7, for example, that doesn't mean there aren't any more moveable seventh chord shapes in the book. Usually, you'll find other moveable voicings for the same chord by looking at other keys throughout the book.

A fingerboard chart of the entire ukulele neck through fret 12 is provided below for reference.

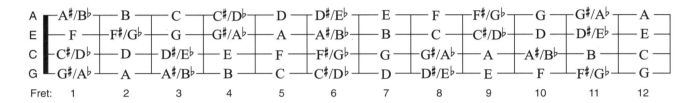

The chords throughout this book are presented in chord grid fashion. In case you're not familiar with this type of notation, below is a detailed explanation of how they're read.

The four vertical lines represent the strings on the ukulele.
The lowest string (G) is on the left, moving through to the highest string (E) on the right.

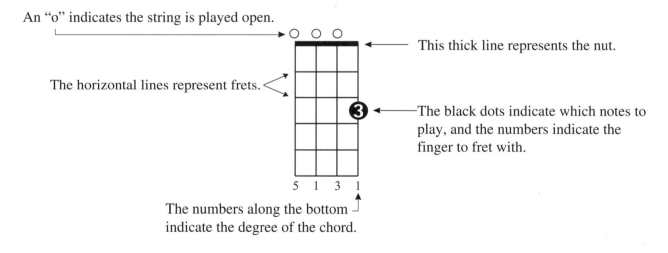

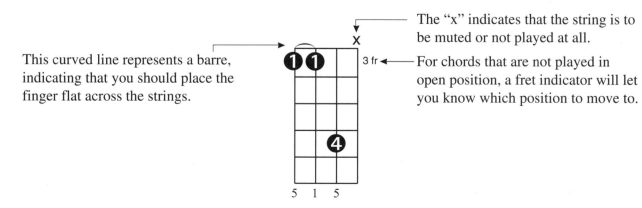

CHORD CONSTRUCTION

This section is intended to provide a basic knowledge of chords, how to build them, and how to use them. Some of you may already know this; if so, skip ahead! If not, read on and learn how to impress your friends who don't know.

TRIADS

A chord is simply a collection of notes deliberately arranged in a harmonious (or sometimes non-harmonious) fashion. The most common type of chord is called a *triad*. The name triad is telling of the number of notes in the chord—three. Triads can be one of four different qualities: major, minor, augmented, or diminished. Below, we find what's known as a C Major triad:

The words "root," "third," and "fifth" below the notes on the staff indicate how each note functions within the chord. A root note is the foundation of the chord and the note after which the chord will be named.

INTERVALS

The other two notes in our C triad (the 3rd and the 5th) are responsible for the *quality* of the chord. The notes C and E are an interval (or distance) of a major 3rd apart. Intervals are comprised of two components: a *number* and a *quality*.

In the case of the number, we can determine that C to E is a *3rd* by simply counting through the musical alphabet. Starting from C: C is one, D is two, and E is three. (The word "root" is many times used interchangeably with the number "1." For all practical purposes, they mean the same thing.) From C to G is a 5th, and we can confirm this by again counting up from C: C(1)–D(2)–E(3)–F(4)–G(5).

Determining the quality of an interval is not quite as easy as the number, but it's not too difficult. It will require a bit of memorization, but it's very logical. Below we'll find all twelve of the notes in the chromatic scale and their intervals measured from a C root note:

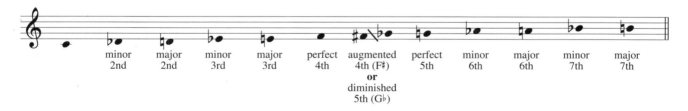

This example tells us a great deal about intervals. We can see a few formulas here at work. The first thing we should notice is that a minor interval is always one half step smaller than a major interval. C to E is a major 3rd, whereas C to E♭ is a minor 3rd. C to A is a major 6th, whereas C to A♭ is a minor 6th, etc. The next thing we should notice is how 4ths and 5ths work. We can see that an augmented interval is always one half step greater than a perfect one, and a diminished interval is always one half step smaller.

Any triad of one of the four above-mentioned qualities will contain a root, 3rd, and 5th. Other types of triads you may encounter include 6 chords, sus4 chords, and sus2 chords. Theses chords are the product of (in the case of sus4 and sus2 chords) replacing the 3rd with another note or (in the case of 6 chords) replacing the 5th (or sometimes adding to it) with another note.

Below are several different qualities of triads which will allow us to examine these intervals at work and note how they affect the names of these chords:

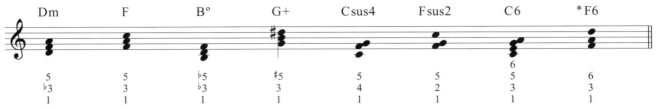

	Dm	F	B°	G+	Csus4	Fsus2	C6	*F6
							6	
	5	5	♭5	♯5	5	5	5	6
	♭3	3	♭3	3	4	2	3	3
	1	1	1	1	1	1	1	1

The symbol ° stands for diminished, while the symbol + stands for augmented.
* Note that the 5th tone may or may not be present in a 6 chord.

7TH CHORDS

Beyond the triad, we'll encounter many more chords, most commonly 7th chords. These chords will not only contain the root, 3rd, and 5th, but also the 7th. Below are a few common 7th chords. (Note that the 7th interval may be major or minor independent of the 3rd, thus affecting the name of the chord.)

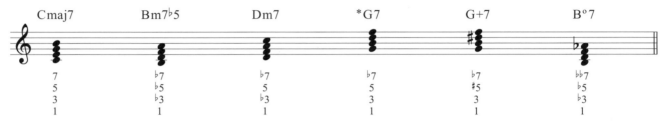

	Cmaj7	Bm7♭5	Dm7	*G7	G+7	B°7
	7	♭7	♭7	♭7	♭7	♭♭7
	5	♭5	5	5	♯5	♭5
	3	♭3	♭3	3	3	♭3
	1	1	1	1	1	1

* Note that the G7 chord contains a major 3rd and a minor 7th. This type of chord is referred to as a *dominant 7th*.

EXTENSIONS

Finally, beyond 7th chords, we have extensions. The concept of extensions is a bit complicated and will only be touched upon here, as it requires more extensive study than is possible within the scope of this book. Basically, extended chords continue the process of stacking notes onto a triad that we began with the 7th chord. Instead of only adding the 7th to the chord, however, in a 9th chord we'll add the 7th and the 9th. In an 11th chord, we'll add the 7th, 9th, and 11th to our triad, etc. Now, here's the catch: not all of the notes need to be present in an extended chord. The general rule is, if the 7th is present, then notes other than the root, 3rd, and 5th are extensions and therefore numbered an octave higher (9, 11, 13). Since we're only capable of playing four notes at a time on the ukulele, we must decide which notes are important and which notes we can omit. Generally speaking, you'll want to include the root, 3rd, 7th, and the extension. The C13 chord below demonstrates this concept:

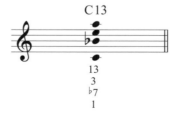

C13
13
3
♭7
1

Note that there is no 5th (G) present in this chord, but the presence of the 7th (B♭) tells us that this chord is called C13, rather than some kind of C6 chord.

Extended chords may contain either the major 3rd or the perfect 11th, but usually not both. These two notes can clash with one another, since the 11th is equivalent to the 4th, only a half step away from the 3rd. In the C13 chord above, the 11th was omitted. In a chord where the 11th is specified, the major 3rd is usually omitted. There may be some cases where your ear tells you it is OK to use a chord with both notes. This book includes examples of both options, with emphasis on the common practice. Minor chords do not have this problem and may include the 11th and minor 3rd together.

INVERSIONS

Since the ukulele only has four strings, chords will often be voiced in *inversion*. A chord is inverted when a note other than the root is in the bass. In a triad, which contains three different notes, there are three basic possibilities for the vertical organization of the notes: root position, first inversion, and second inversion. Chords in root position contain the root of the chord in the bass; in other words, they are not inversions. A first inversion chord, however, contains the 3rd in the bass, while a second inversion chord contains the 5th in the bass. This is demonstrated below:

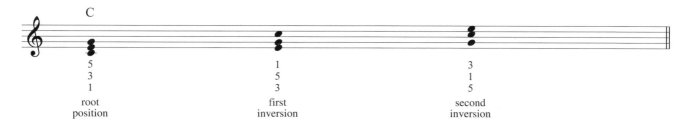

In a seventh chord or an extended chord, which contains four different notes, we have another inversion possibility. In addition to the first and second inversions, we can also have a third inversion, which places the 7th of the chord in the bass.

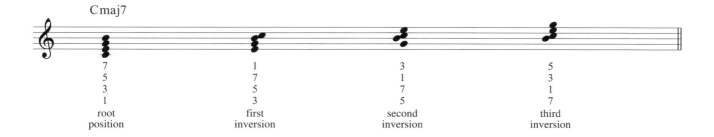

Occasionally, extended chords will feature an extension (9th, 11th, or 13th) in the bass. While these chords are inversions as well, they aren't typically numbered as with the triads and seventh chords. For instance, the chord below would most likely be called "D9 with E in the bass," or "D9 with the 9th in the bass," or simply "D9 over E."

Again, this section is intended to be a basic tutorial on the concept of chord construction and chord theory. If you're interested in furthering your knowledge on this subject, I suggest you take a look at some of the many books dedicated to chord construction and theory.

CHORD QUALITIES

Below is a list of the twenty-eight different chord qualities presented in this book, their abbreviations, and their formulas:

CHORD TYPE	ABBREVIATION	FORMULA
Major	C	1–3–5
Minor	Cm	1–♭3–5
Augmented	C+	1–3–♯5
Diminished	C°	1–♭3–♭5
Fifth (Power Chord)	C5	1–5
Added Ninth	Cadd9	1–3–5–9
Minor Added Ninth	Cm(add9)	1–♭3–5–9
Suspended Fourth	Csus4	1–4–5
Suspended Second	Csus2	1–2–5
Sixth	C6	1–3–5–6
Minor Sixth	Cm6	1–♭3–5–6
Major Seventh	Cmaj7	1–3–5–7
Major Ninth	Cmaj9	1–3–5–7–9
Minor Seventh	Cm7	1–♭3–5–♭7
Minor, Major Seventh	Cm(maj7)	1–♭3–5–7
Minor Seventh, Flat Fifth	Cm7♭5	1–♭3–♭5–♭7
Minor Ninth	Cm9	1–♭3–5–♭7–9
Minor Eleventh	Cm11	1–♭3–5–♭7–9–11
Seventh	C7	1–3–5–♭7
Seventh, Suspended Fourth	C7sus4	1–4–5–♭7
Augmented Seventh	C+7	1–3–♯5–♭7
Seventh, Flat Fifth	C7♭5	1–3–♭5–♭7
Ninth	C9	1–3–5–♭7–9
Seventh, Sharp Ninth	C7♯9	1–3–5–♭7–♯9
Seventh, Flat Ninth	C7♭9	1–3–5–♭7–♭9
Eleventh	C11	1–3–5–♭7–9–11*
Thirteenth	C13	1–3–5–♭7–9–11–13 **
Diminished Seventh	C°7	1–♭3–♭5–♭♭7

* The 3rd is sometimes omitted from an eleventh chord.
** The 11th is sometimes omitted from a thirteenth chord.

DGBE=G

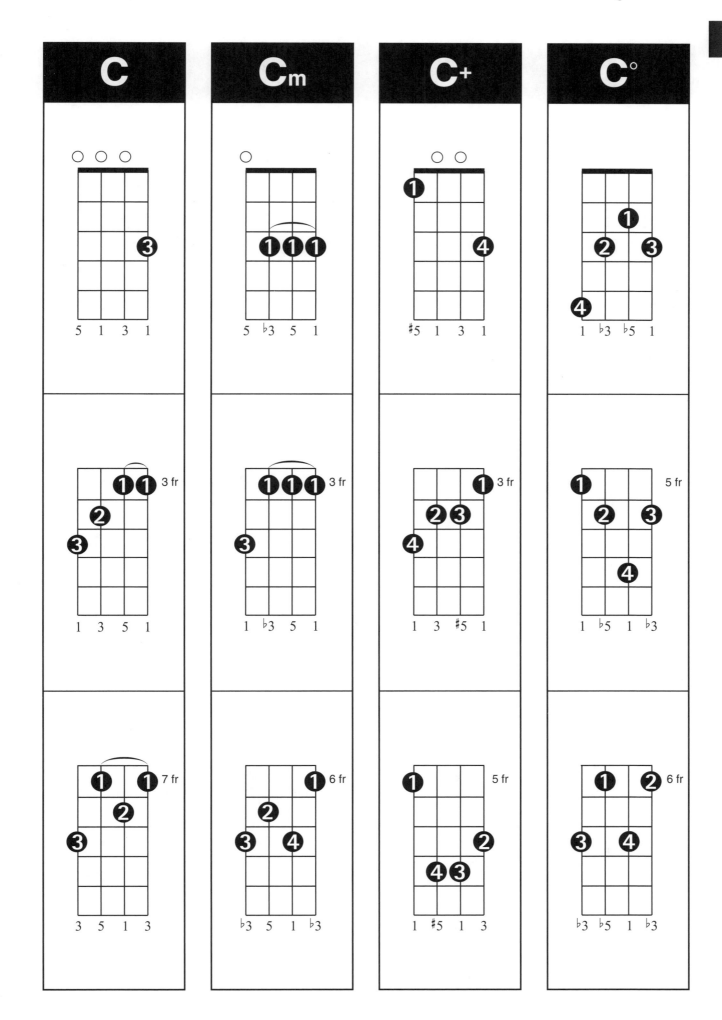

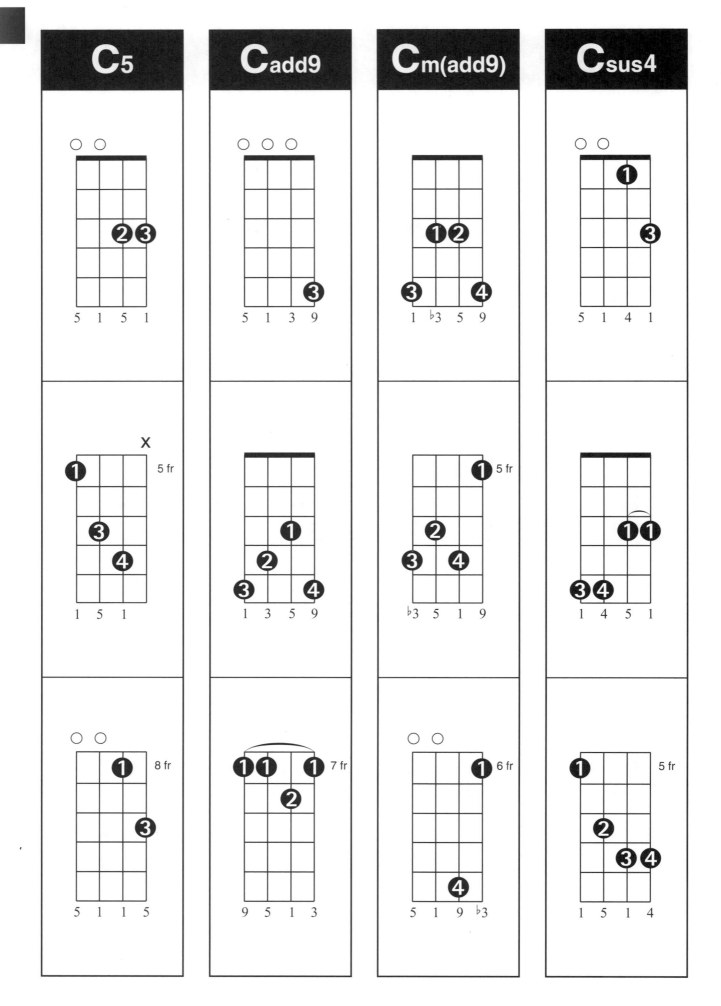

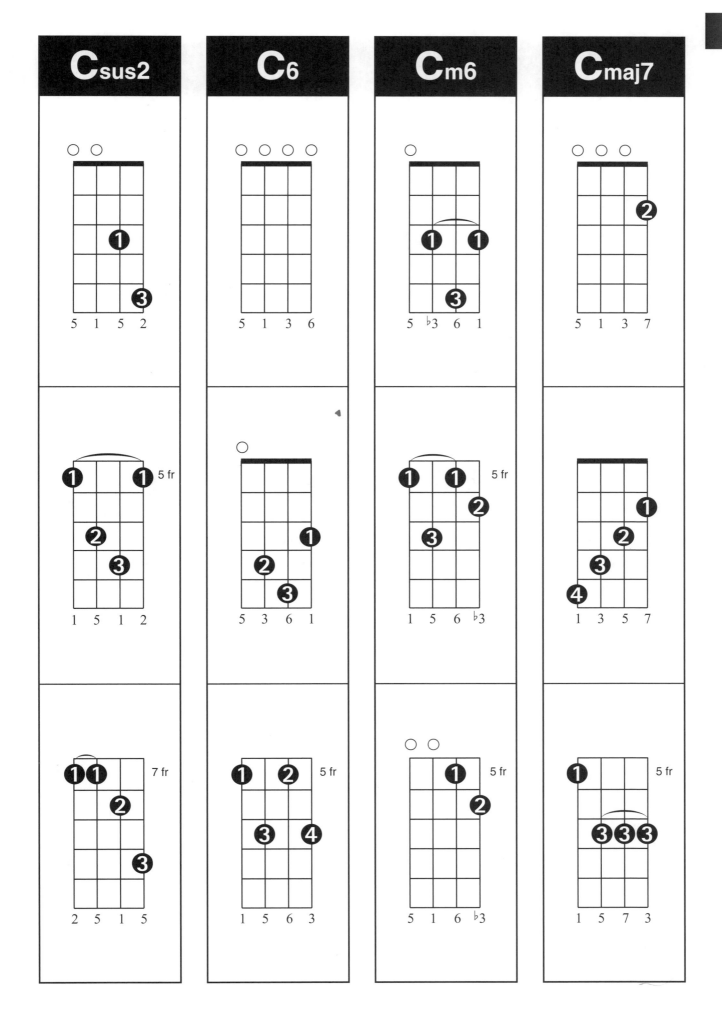

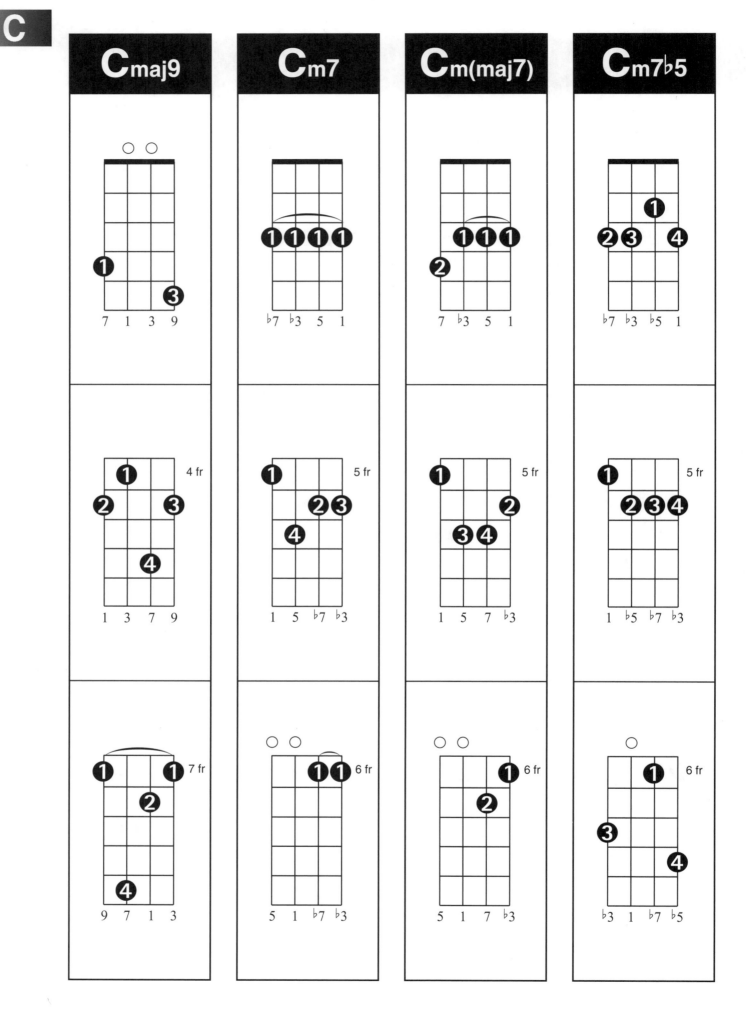

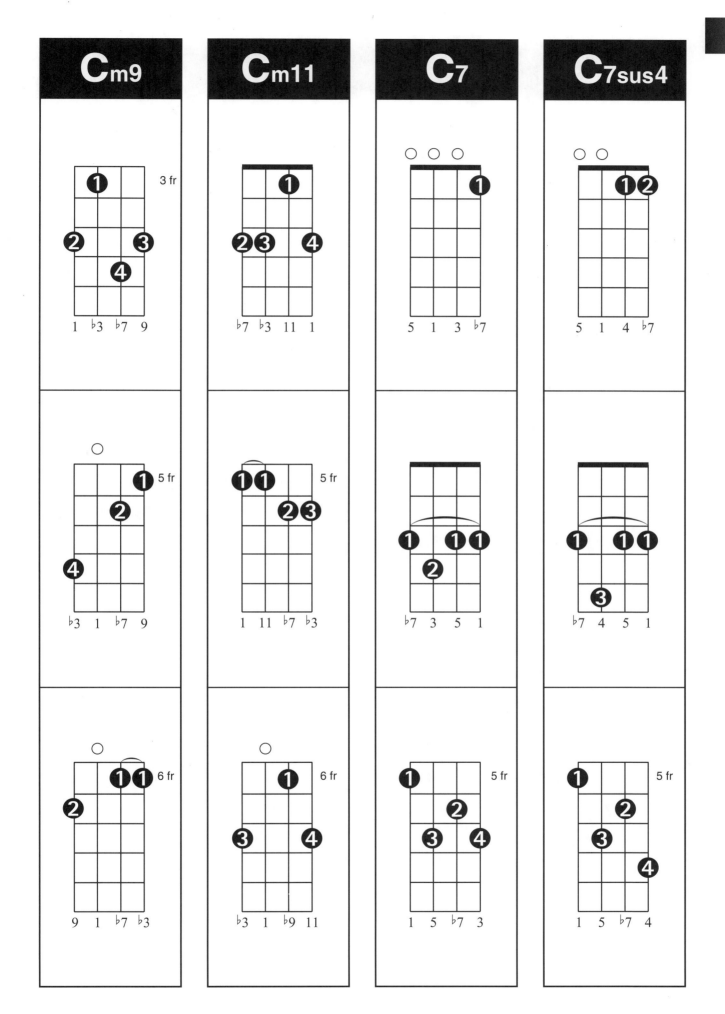

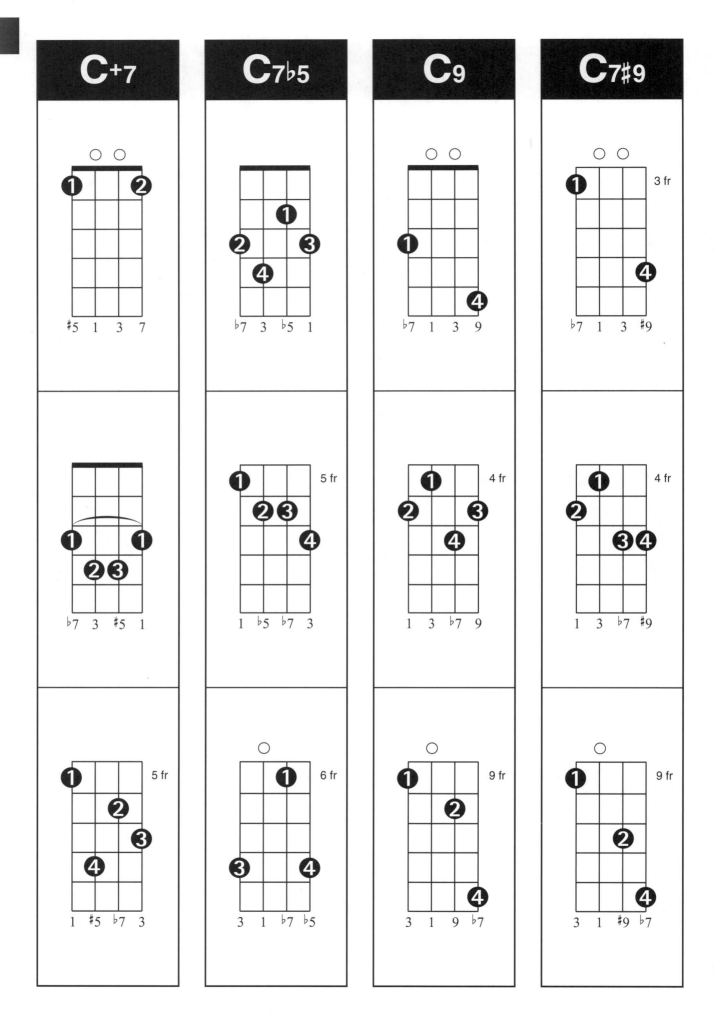

C+7

C7♭5

C9

C7♯9

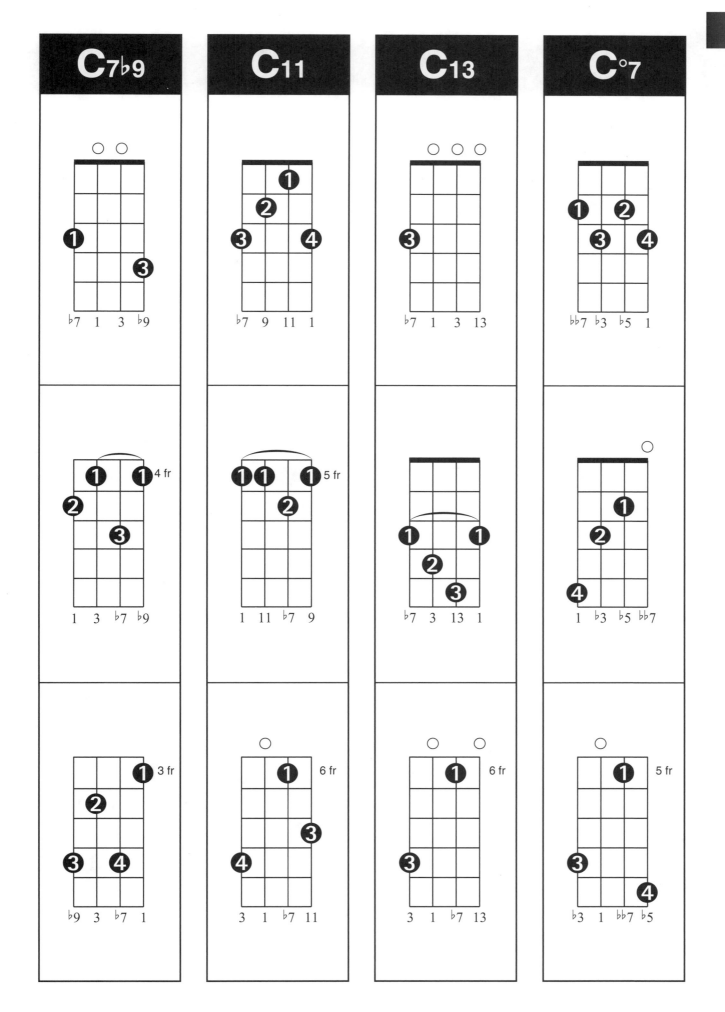

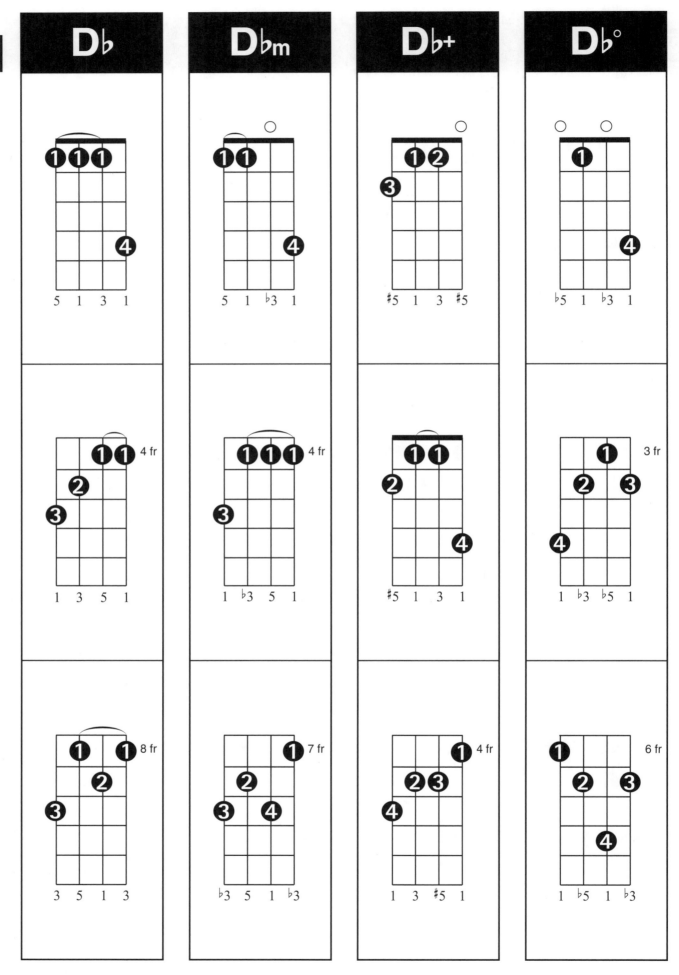

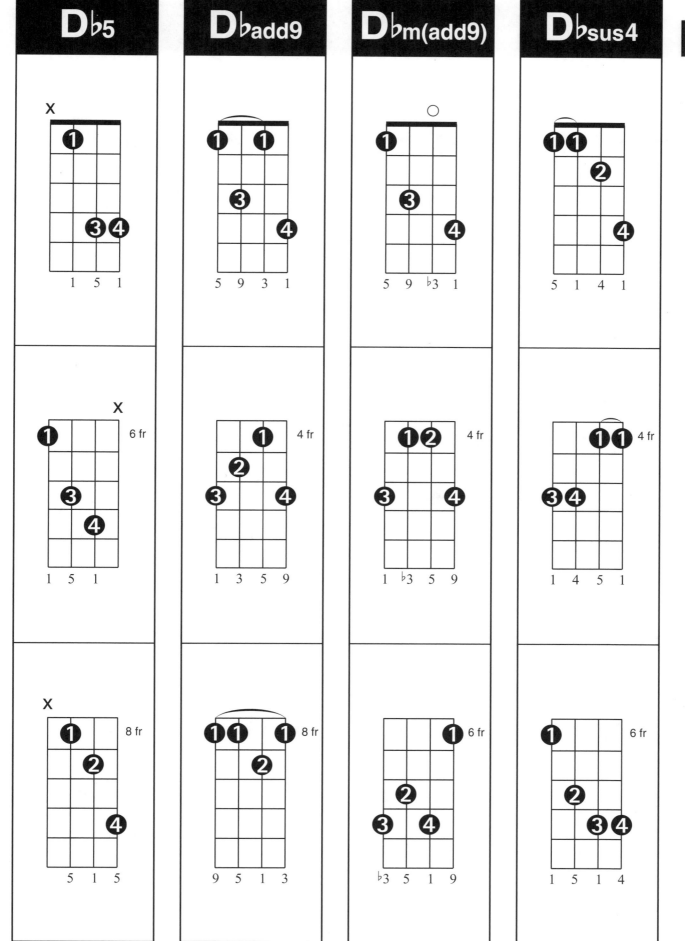

D♭5 D♭add9 D♭m(add9) D♭sus4

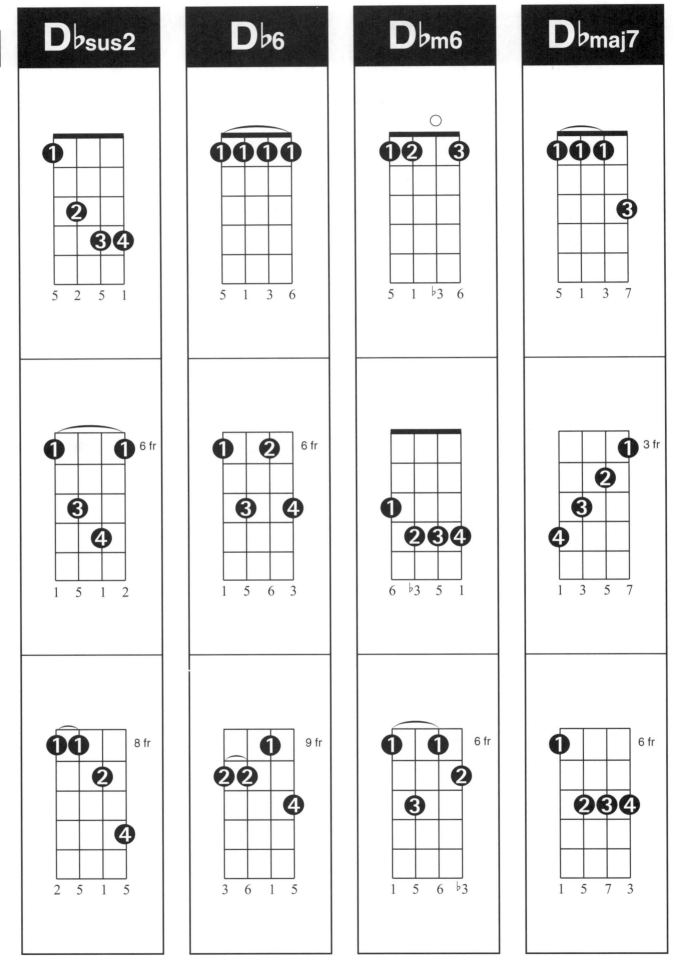

D♭maj9

D♭m7

D♭m(maj7)

D♭m7♭5

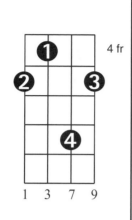

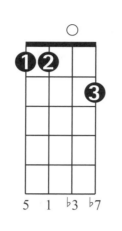

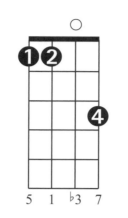

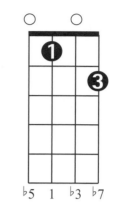

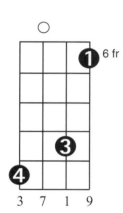

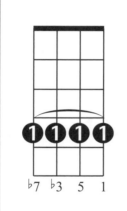

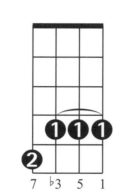

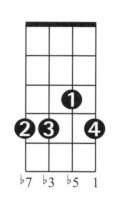

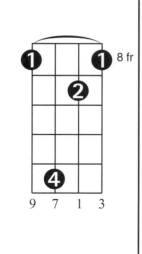

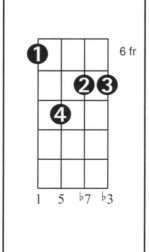

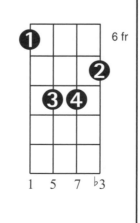

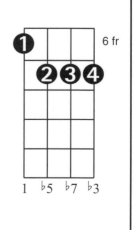

19

Dbm9

○

1

2   3

♭7 9 ♭3 1

1

2   3
   4

1 ♭3 ♭7 9

4 fr

1

2

3

4

9 ♭7 1 ♭3

7 fr

Dbm11

1

2 3   4

♭7 ♭3 11 1

○

1   2

4

♭7 11 ♭3 1

4 fr

1 2

3 4

1 11 ♭7 ♭3

6 fr

Db7

1 1 1
        2

5 1 3 ♭7

1   1 1
  2

♭7 3 5 1

4 fr

1

2

3   4

1 5 ♭7 3

6 fr

Db7sus4

1 1
      2 3

5 1 4 ♭7

1   1 1
  3

♭7 4 5 1

4 fr

1

2

3

4

1 5 ♭7 4

6 fr

20

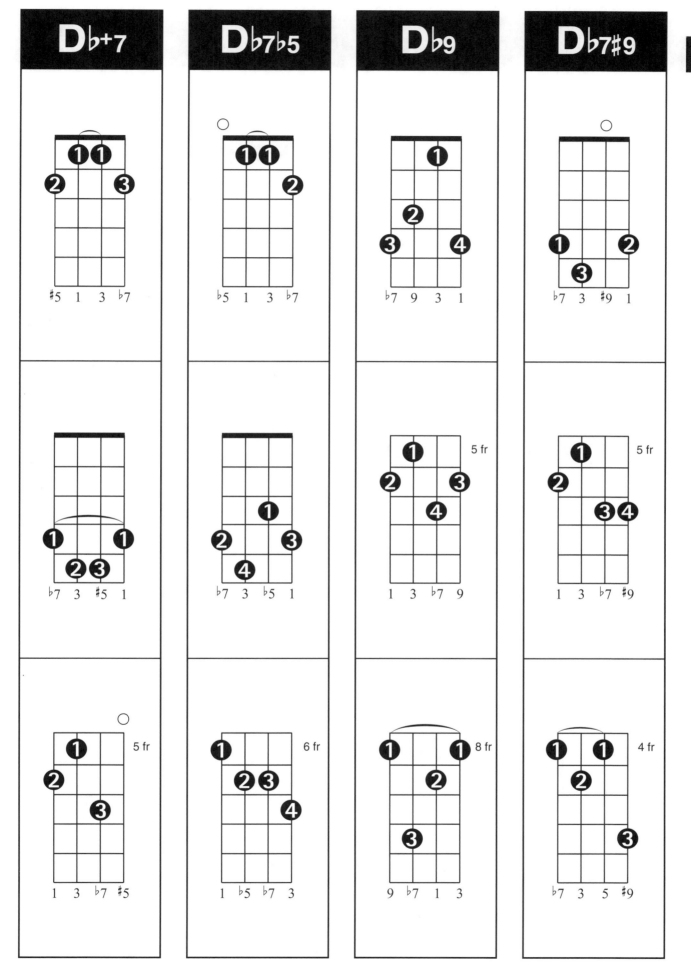

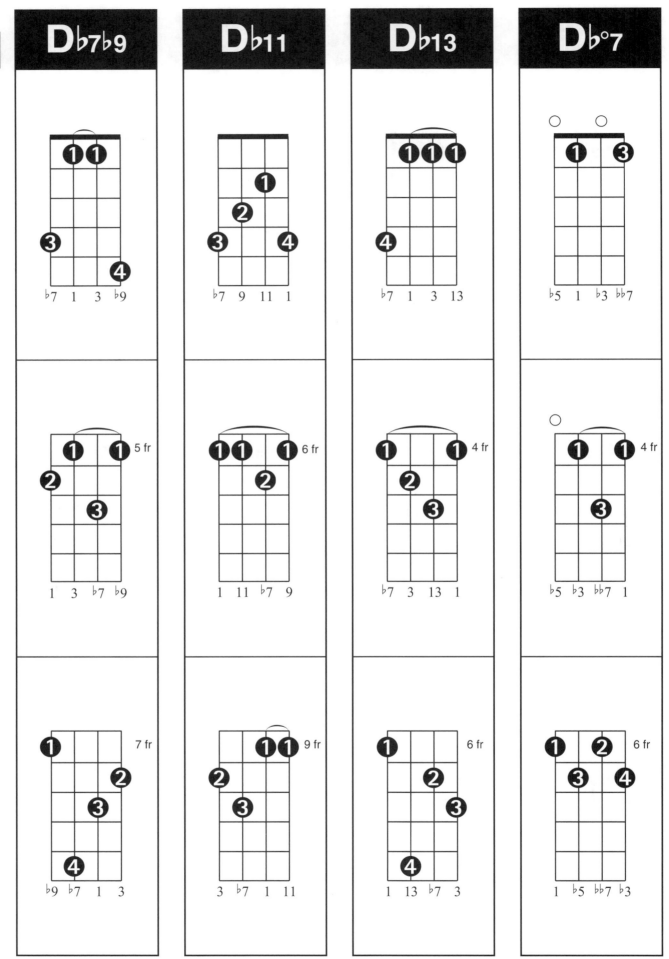

DG-BE= A

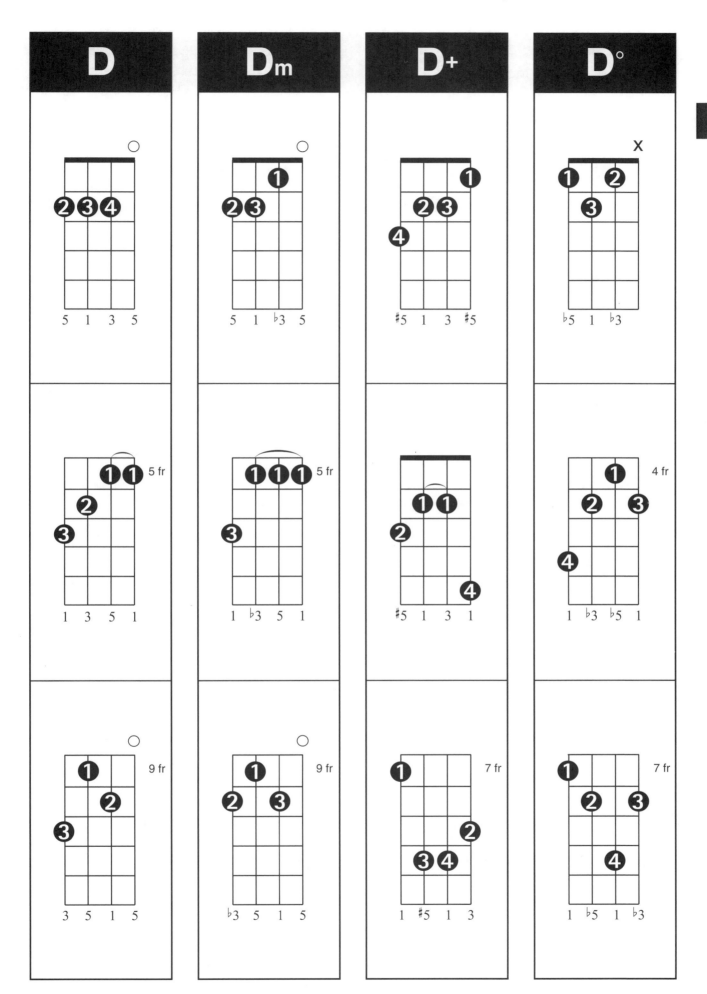

D5 | Dadd9 | Dm(add9) | Dsus4

D5

X

① ③④

1 5 1

○ 7 fr
① ③ ④

1 5 1 5

X 9 fr
① ② ④

5 1 5

Dadd9

① ① ③ ④

5 9 3 1

5 fr
① ② ③ ④

1 3 5 9

○ 6 fr
① ③ ④

9 3 1 5

Dm(add9)

①② 5 fr
③ ④

1 ♭3 5 9

○ 5 fr
① ③ ④

9 ♭3 1 5

① 7 fr
② ③ ④

♭3 5 1 9

Dsus4

○   ○
① ②

4 1 4 5

①① ② ④

5 1 4 1

①① 5 fr
③④

1 4 5 1

24

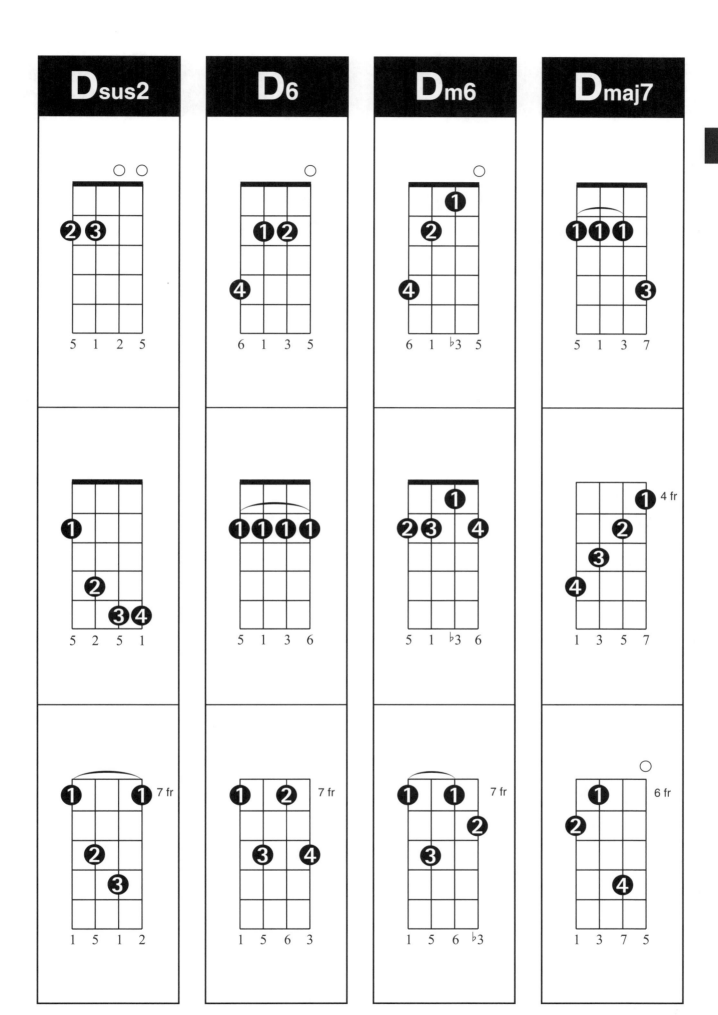

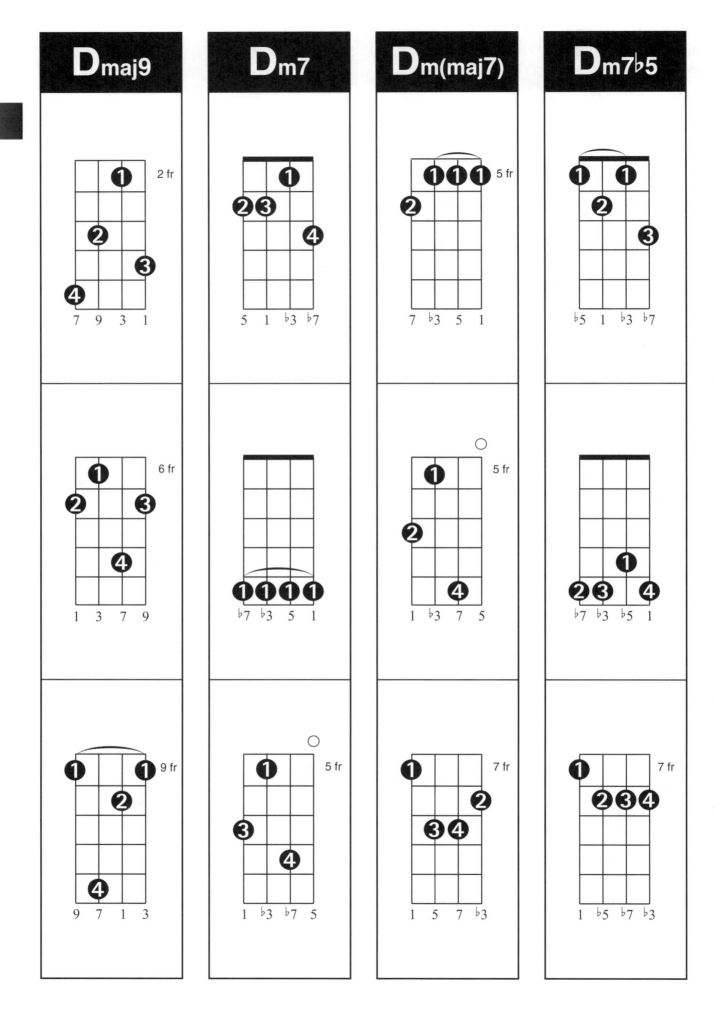

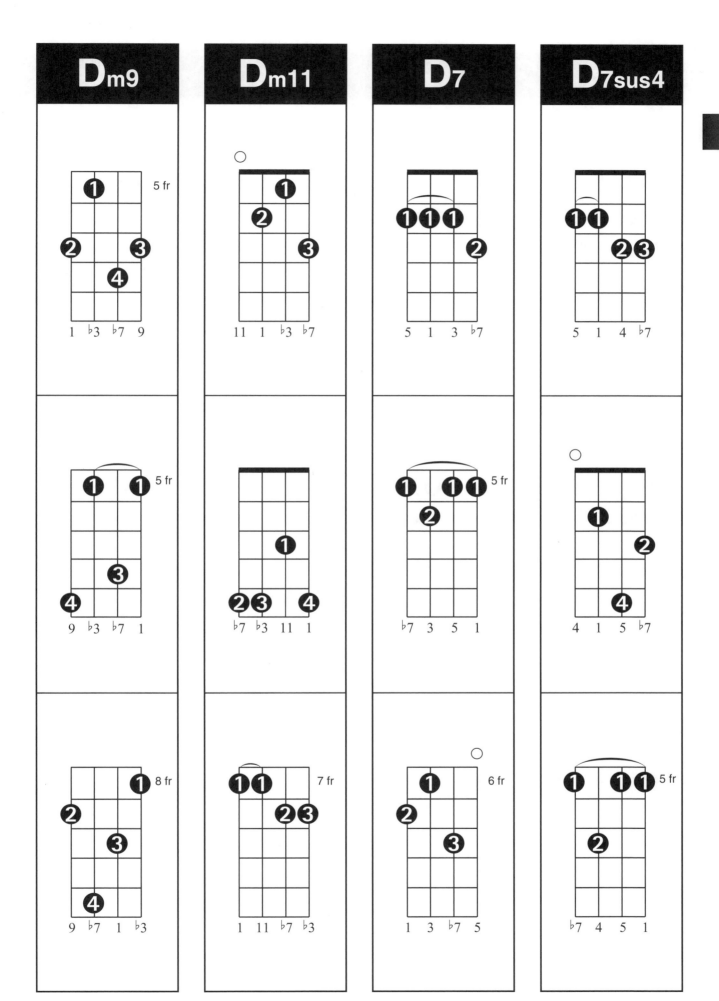

D+7

#5 1 3 b7

5 fr
b7 3 #5 1

7 fr
1 #5 b7 3

D7b5

b5 1 3 b7

4 fr
b7 3 b5 1

7 fr
1 b5 b7 3

D9

b7 9 3 1

5 fr
b7 3 9 1

6 fr
1 3 b7 9

D7#9

5 fr
b7 3 5 #9

6 fr
1 3 b7 #9

9 fr
#9 b7 1 3

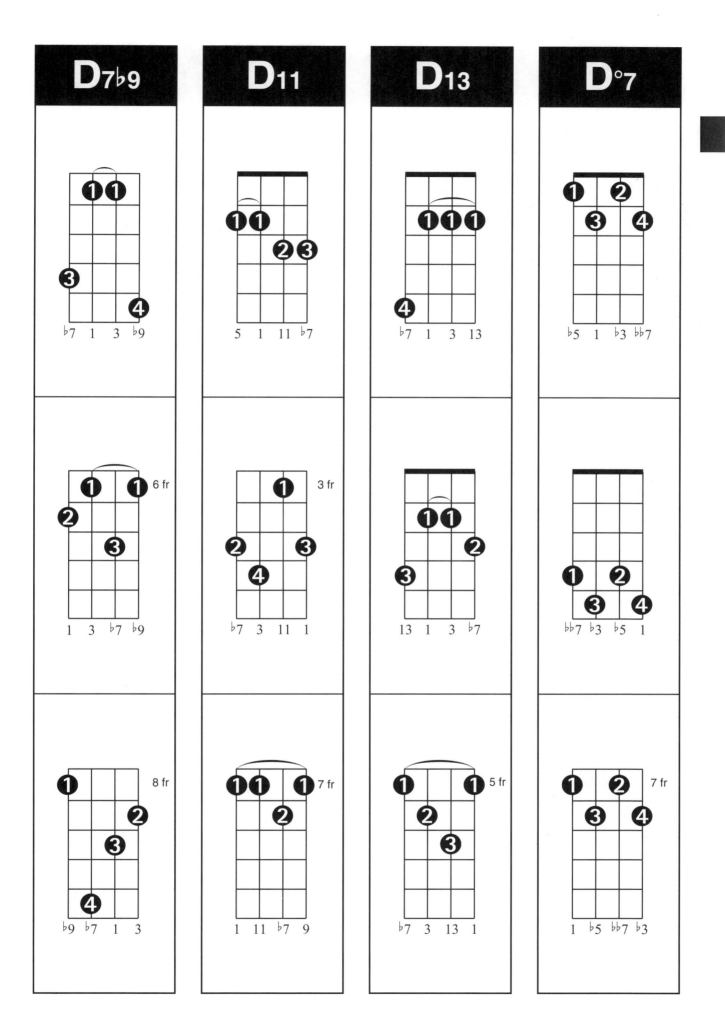

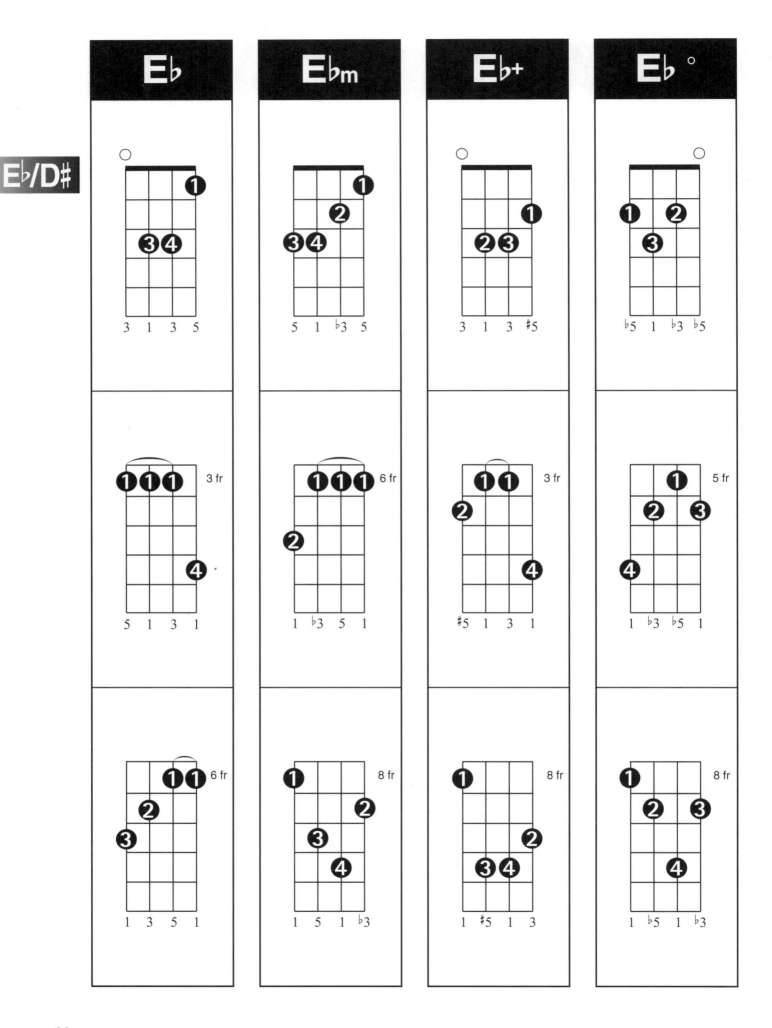

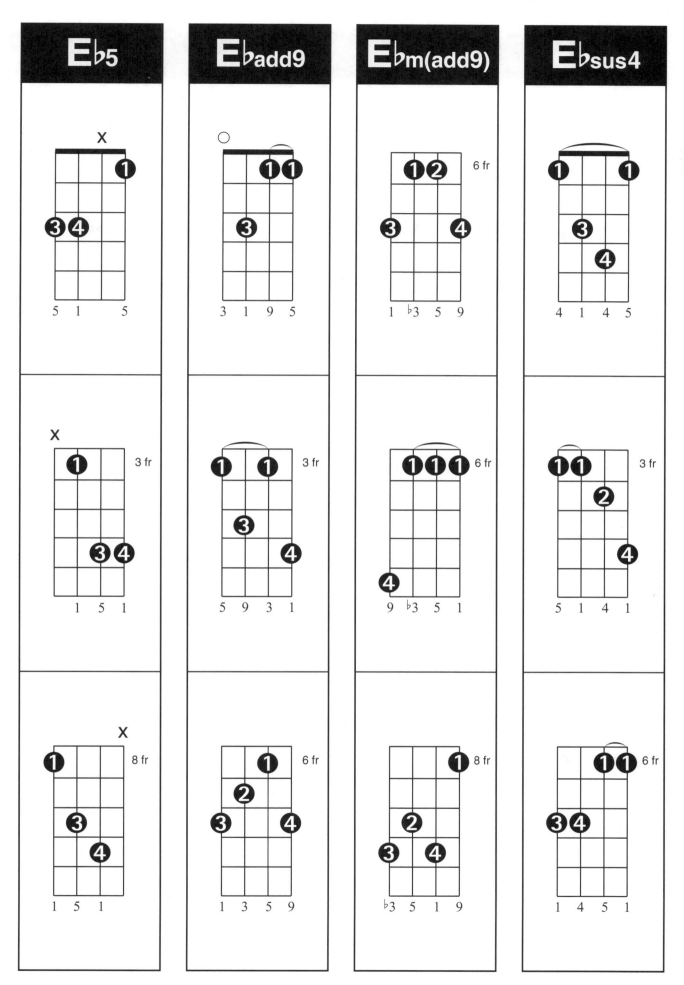

Eb/D#

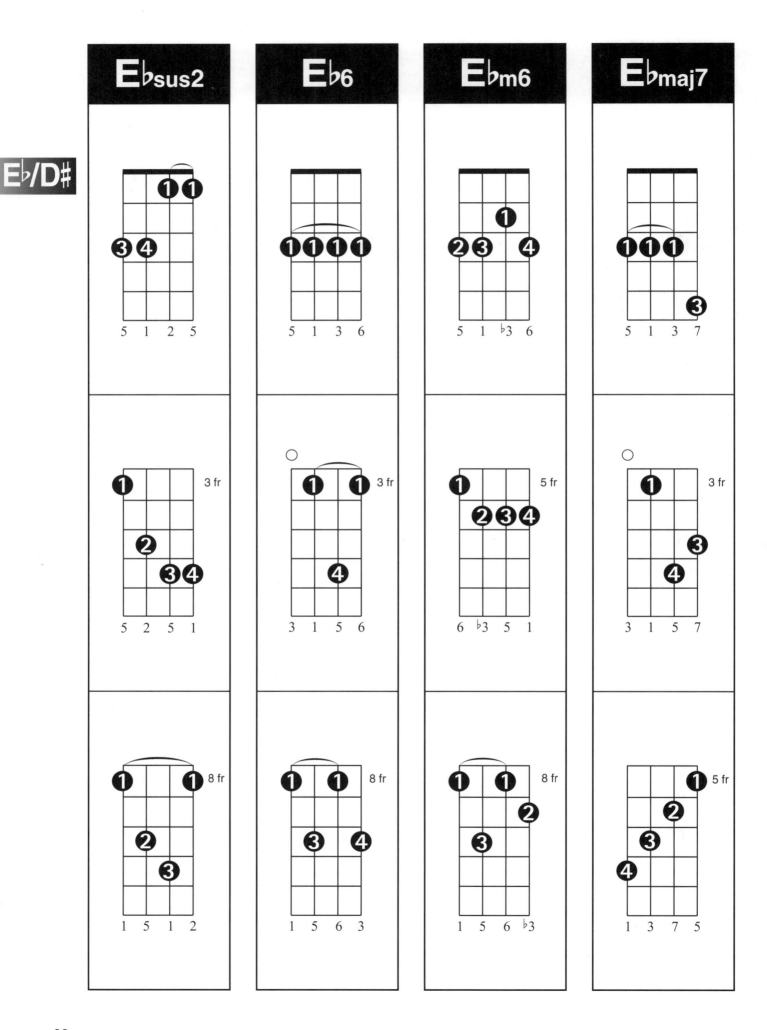

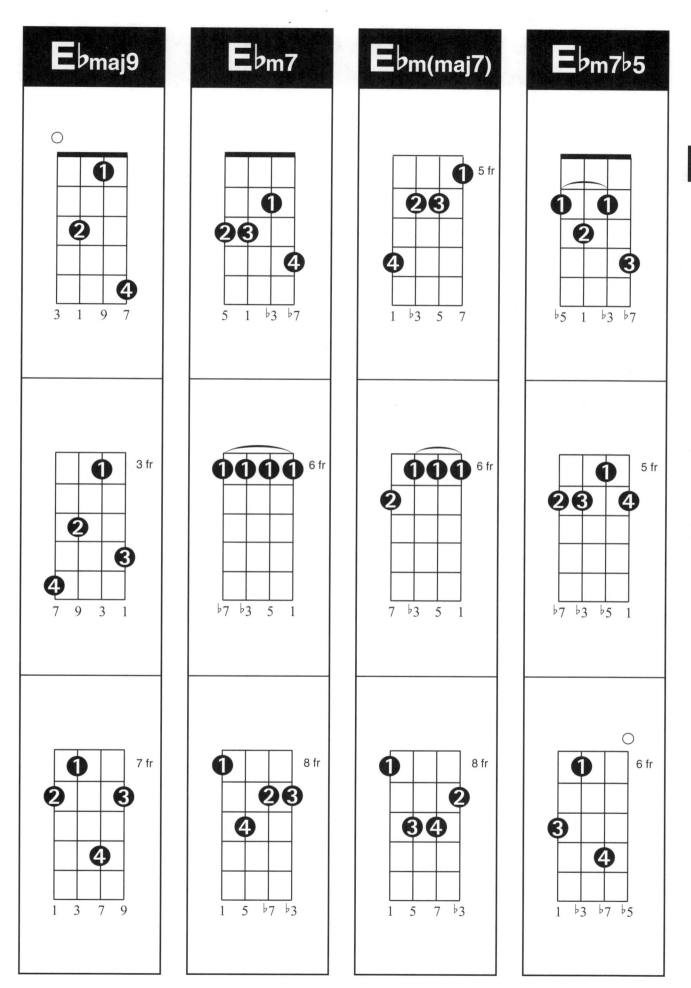

Ebm9

6 fr

①

② ③

④

1 ♭3 ♭7 9

6 fr

① ①

④

③

9 ♭3 ♭7 1

9 fr

①

②

③

④

9 ♭7 1 ♭3

Ebm11

①

②

③

④

11 1 ♭3 ♭7

4 fr

①

② ③ ④

♭7 ♭3 11 1

8 fr

① ①

② ③

1 11 ♭7 ♭3

Eb7

① ① ①

②

5 1 3 ♭7

○

3 fr

①

②

④

3 1 5 ♭7

8 fr

①

②

③ ④

1 5 ♭7 3

Eb7sus4

① ①

② ③

5 1 4 ♭7

6 fr

① ① ①

②

♭7 4 5 1

8 fr

①

②

③

④

1 5 ♭7 4

34

E♭+7

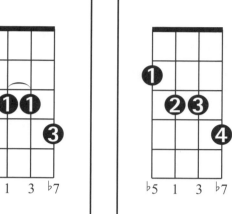

#5   1   3   ♭7

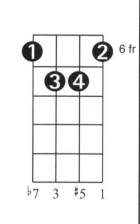

6 fr

♭7   3   #5   1

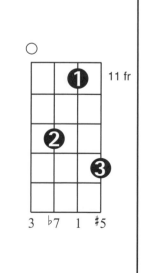

11 fr

3   ♭7   1   #5

E♭7♭5

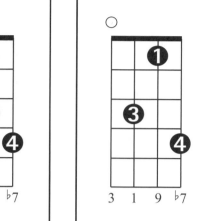

♭5   1   3   ♭7

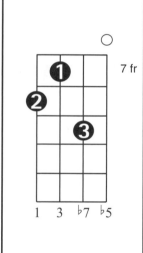

7 fr

1   3   ♭7   ♭5

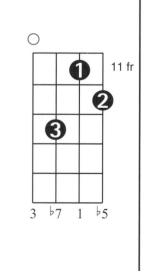

11 fr

3   ♭7   1   ♭5

E♭9

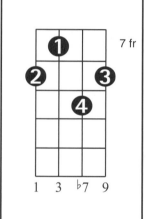

3   1   9   ♭7

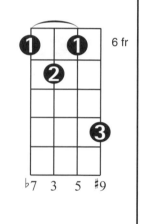

7 fr

1   3   ♭7   9

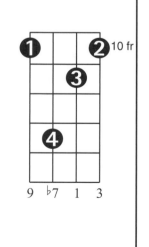

10 fr

9   ♭7   1   3

E♭7#9

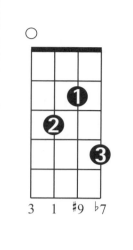

3   1   #9   ♭7

6 fr

♭7   3   5   #9

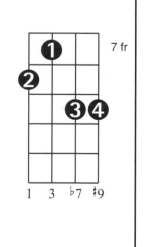

7 fr

1   3   ♭7   #9

E♭7♭9

3 fr

3 1 ♭9 ♭7

♭7 1 3 ♭9

7 fr

1 3 ♭7 ♭9

E♭11

5 1 11 ♭7

11 1 9 ♭7

8 fr

1 11 ♭7 9

E♭13

3 fr

♭7 1 3 13

6 fr

♭7 3 13 1

11 fr

3 ♭7 1 13

E♭°7

♭5 1 ♭3 ♭♭7

♭♭7 1 ♭3 ♭5

8 fr

1 ♭5 ♭♭7 ♭3

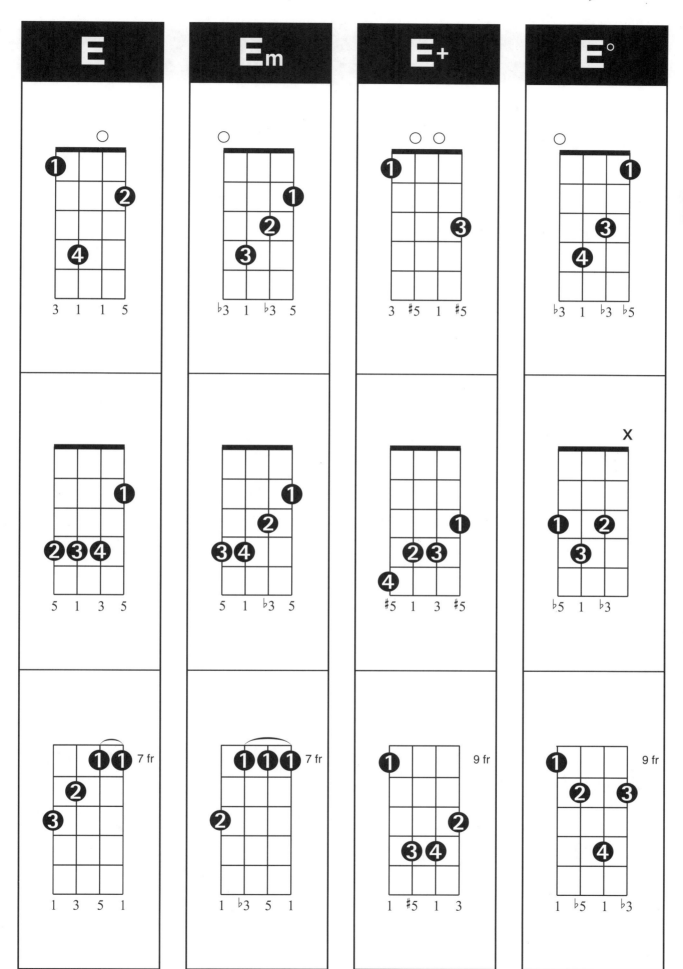

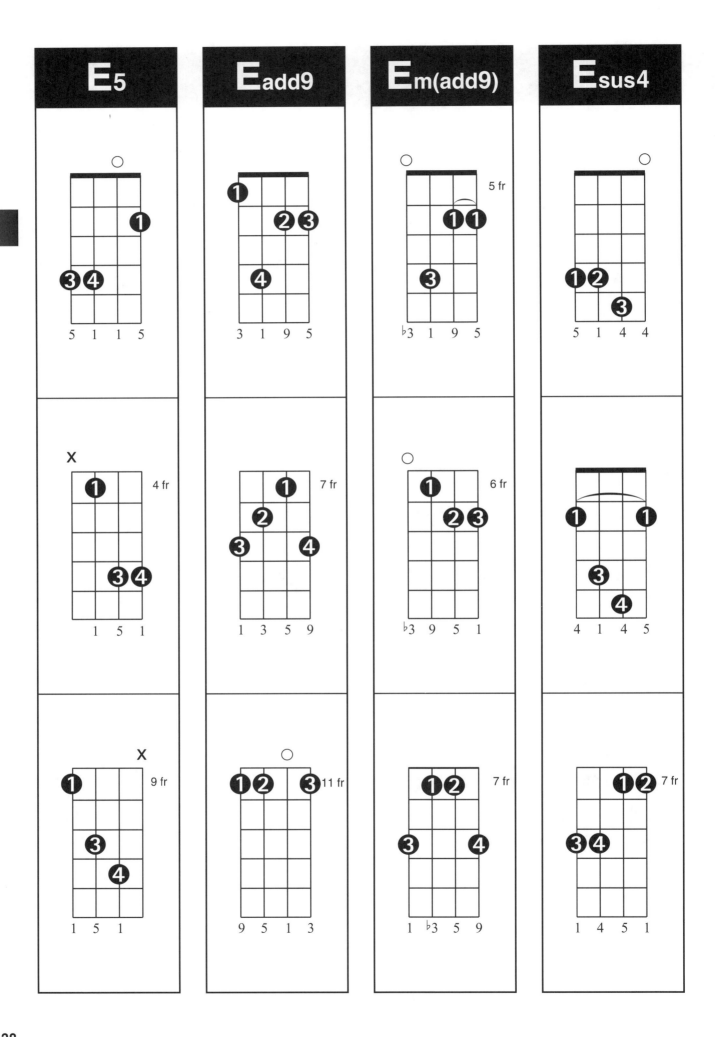

E5   Eadd9   Em(add9)   Esus4

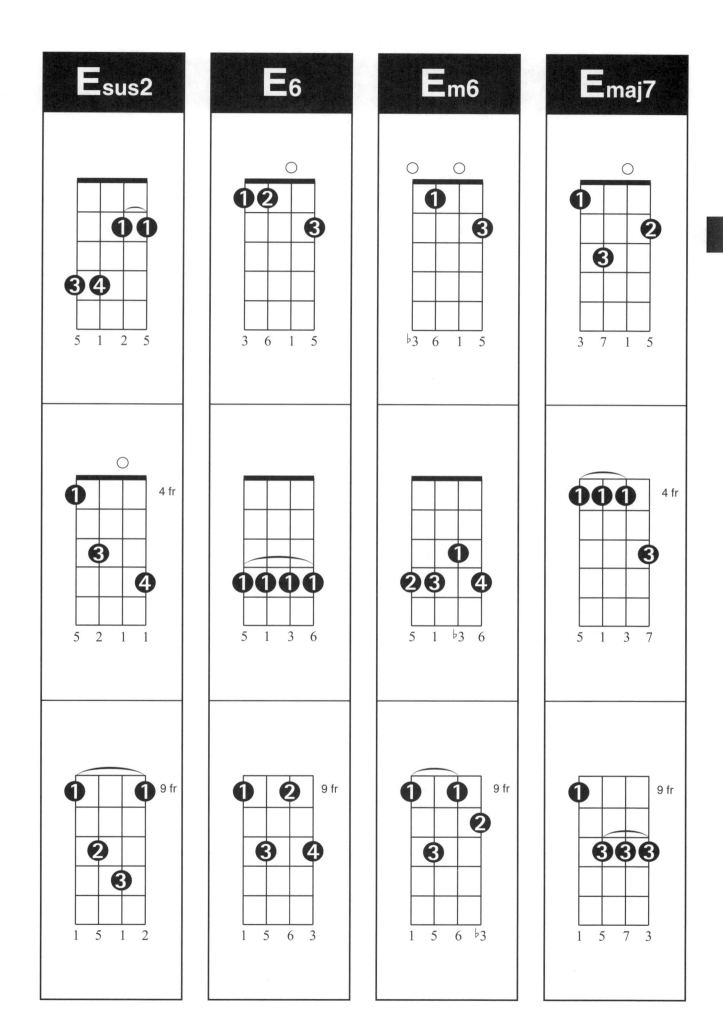

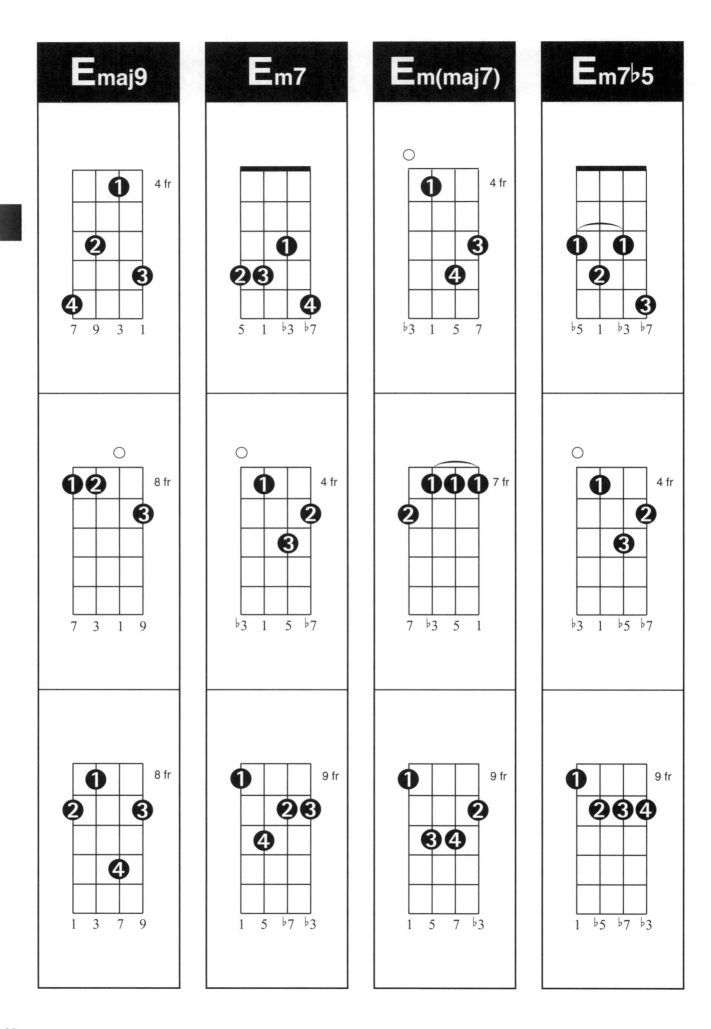

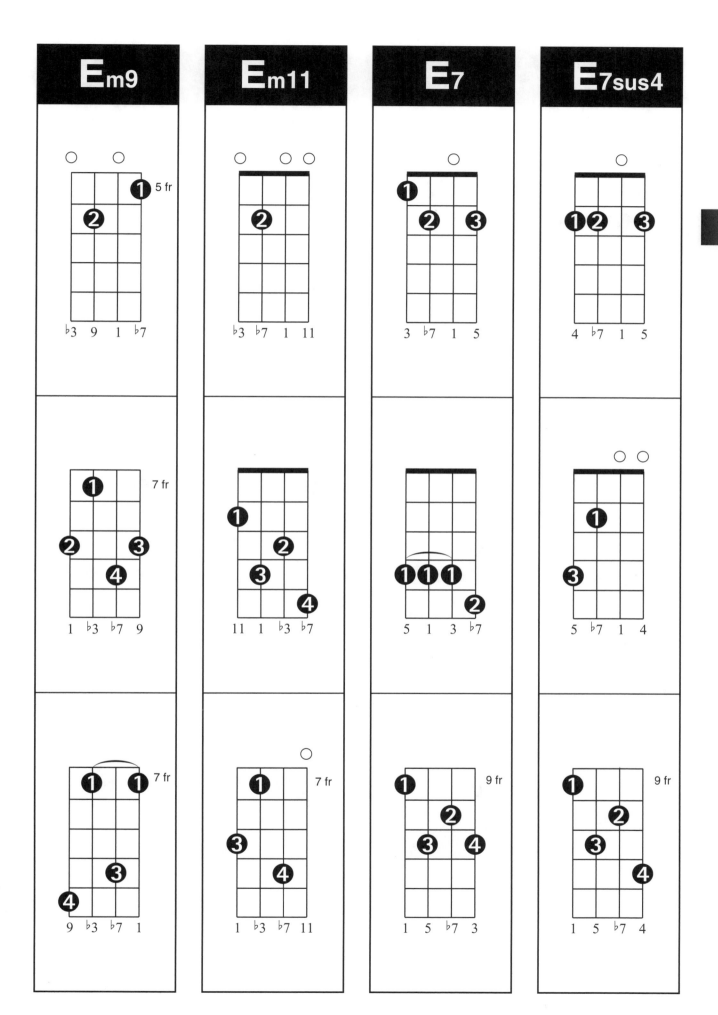

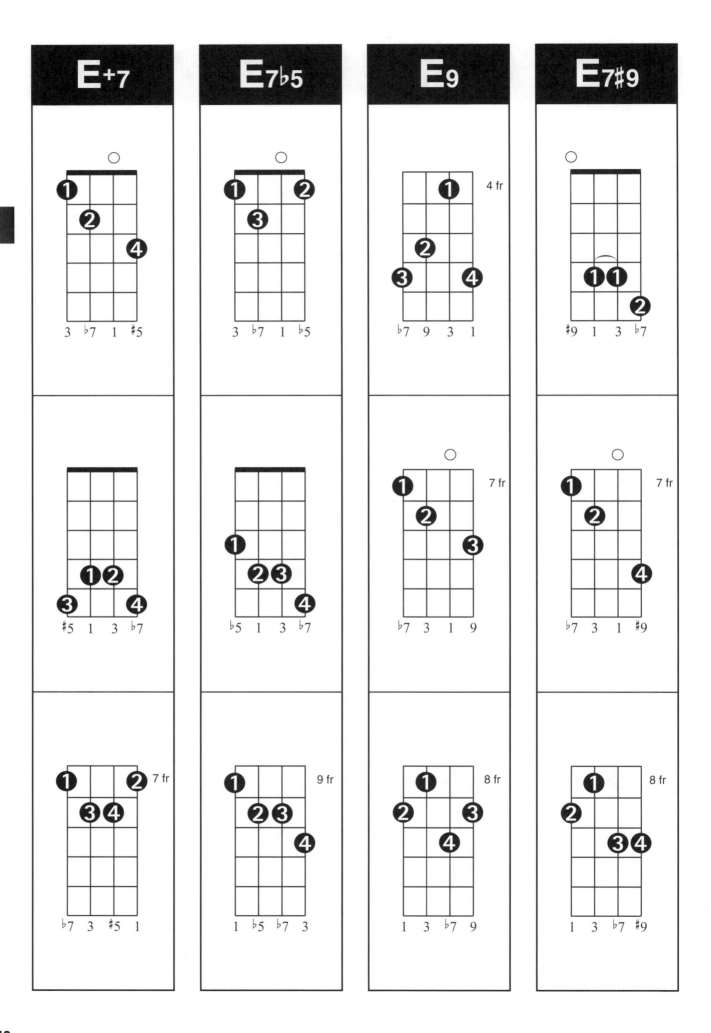

E+7   E7♭5   E9   E7♯9

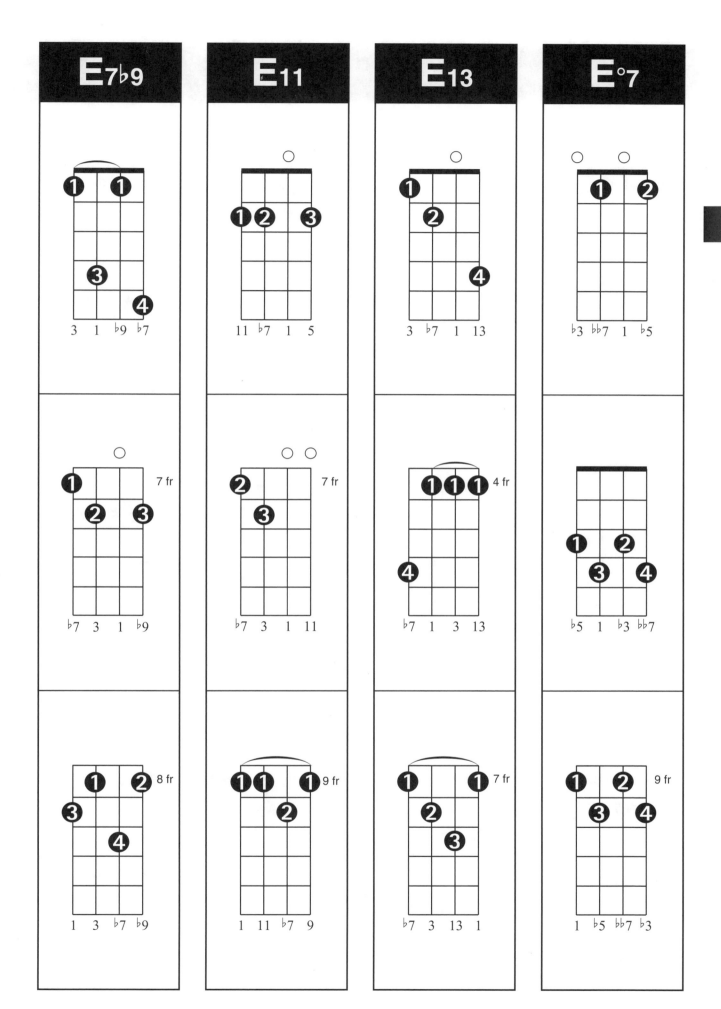

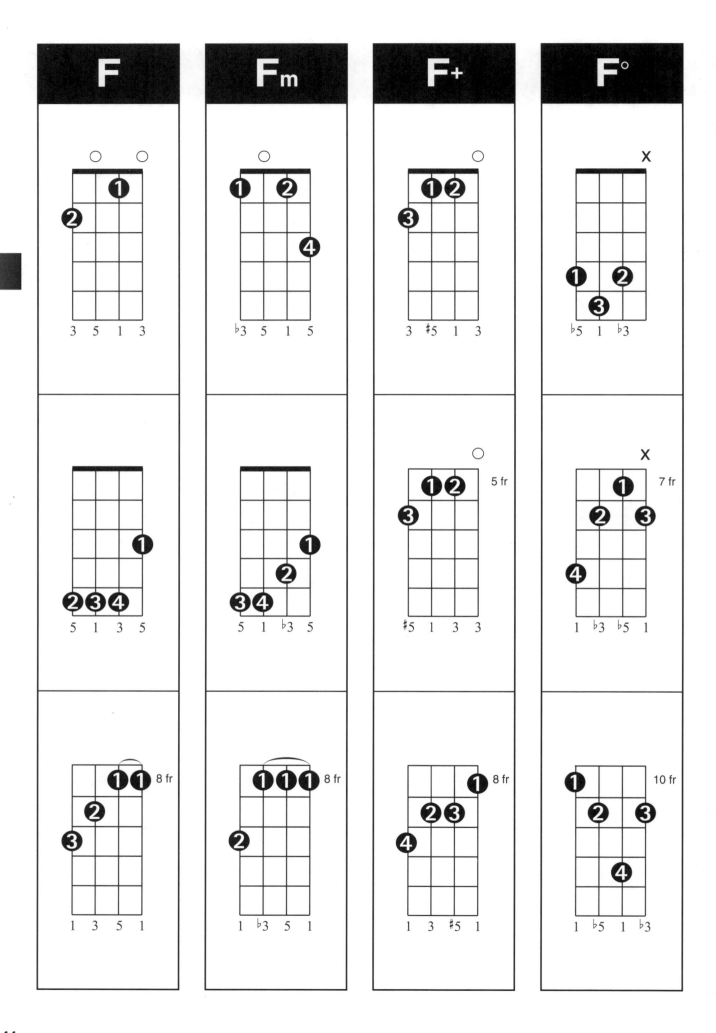

DGBE=C.

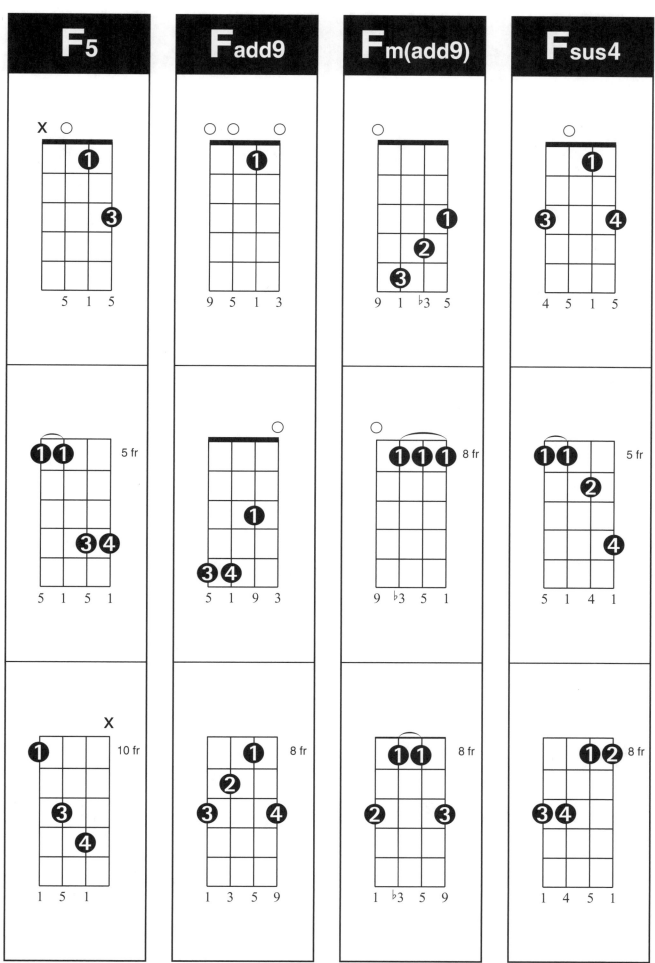

F

F sus2

Open position:
Frets (top): ○ ○

Fingers: 1, 3

Notes: 2 5 1 5

Position 2:
Fingers: 1 1, 3 4

Notes: 5 1 2 5

Position 3 (10 fr):
Fingers: 1 1, 2, 3

Notes: 1 5 1 2

F 6

Open position:
Fingers: 1, 2 3, 4

Notes: 3 6 1 5

Position 2:
Fingers: 1 1 1 1

Notes: 5 1 3 6

Position 3 (10 fr):
Frets (top): ○
Fingers: 1, 2, 3

Notes: 1 5 6 3

F m6

Open position:
Fingers: 1 1, 2, 3

Notes: ♭3 6 1 5

Position 2:
Fingers: 1, 2 3, 4

Notes: 5 1 ♭3 6

Position 3 (10 fr):
Fingers: 1 1, 2, 3

Notes: 1 5 6 ♭3

F maj7

Open position:
Fingers: 1, 2, 3, 4

Notes: 3 7 1 5

Position 2 (5 fr):
Frets (top): ○
Fingers: 1, 3, 4

Notes: 7 1 5 3

Position 3 (7 fr):
Fingers: 1, 2, 3, 4

Notes: 1 3 5 7

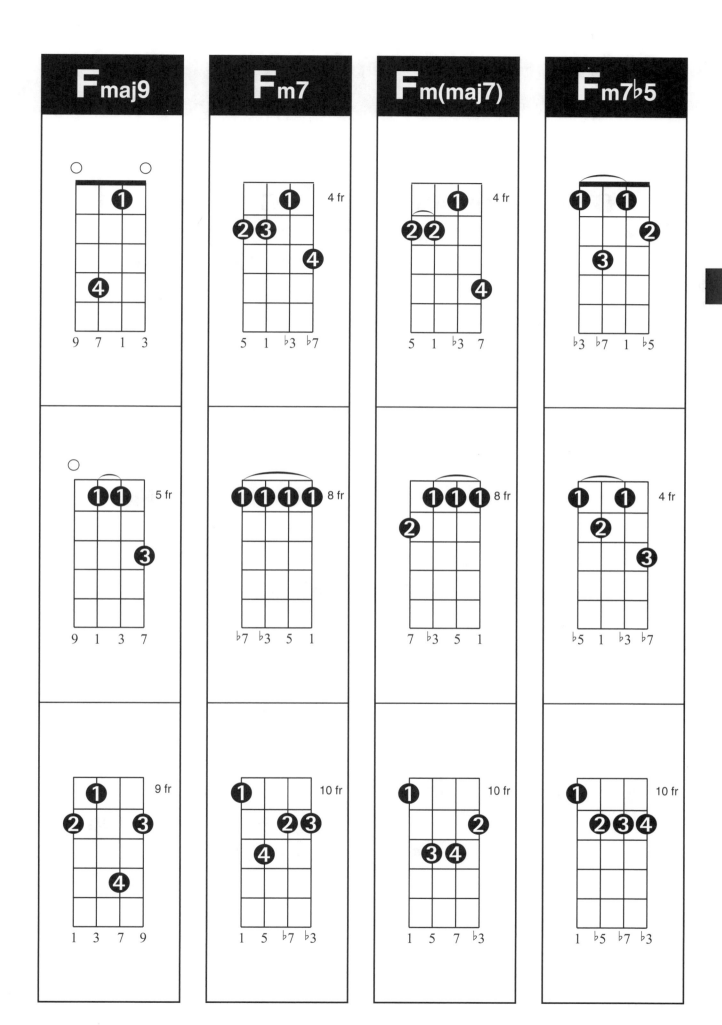

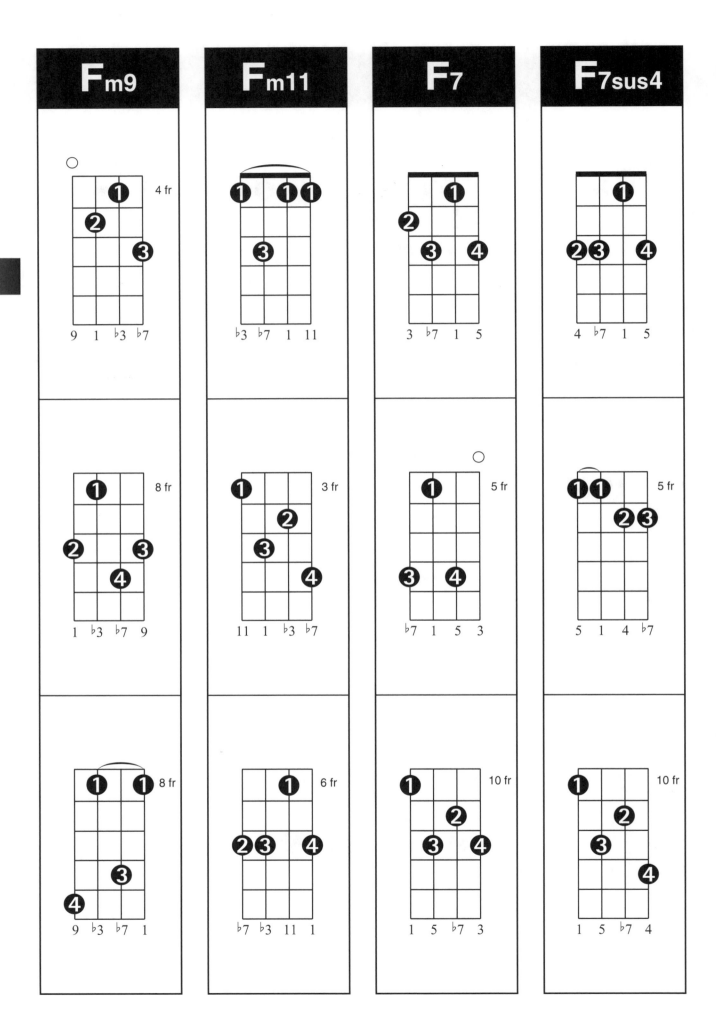

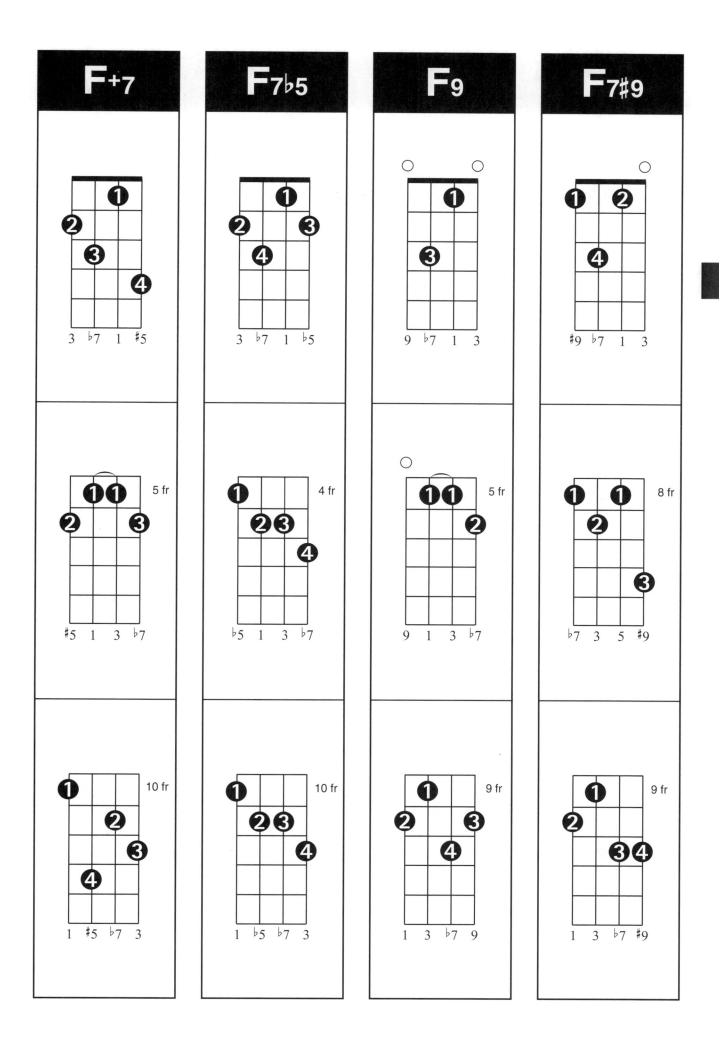

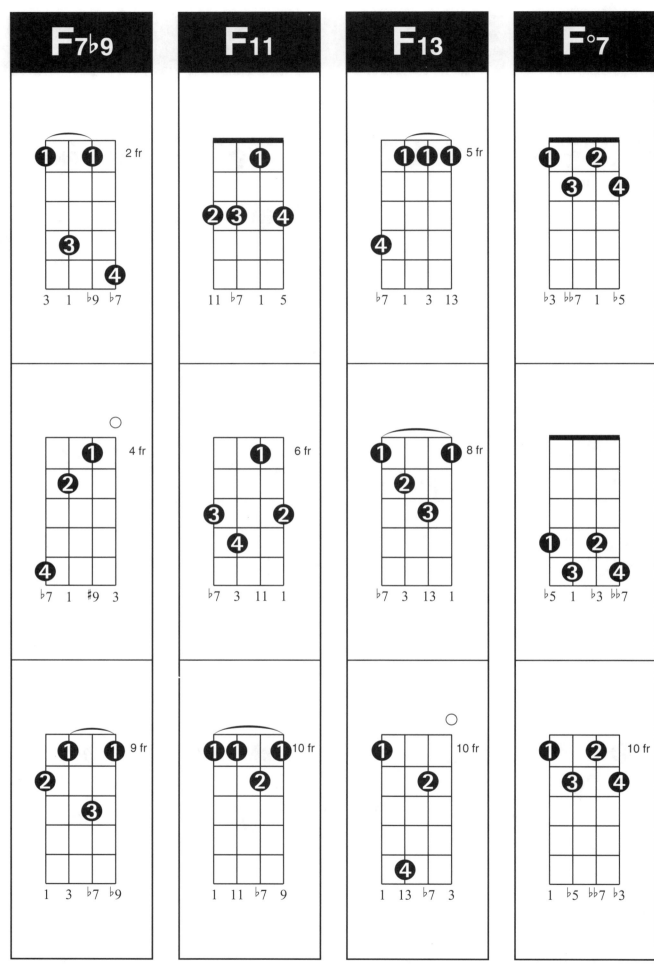

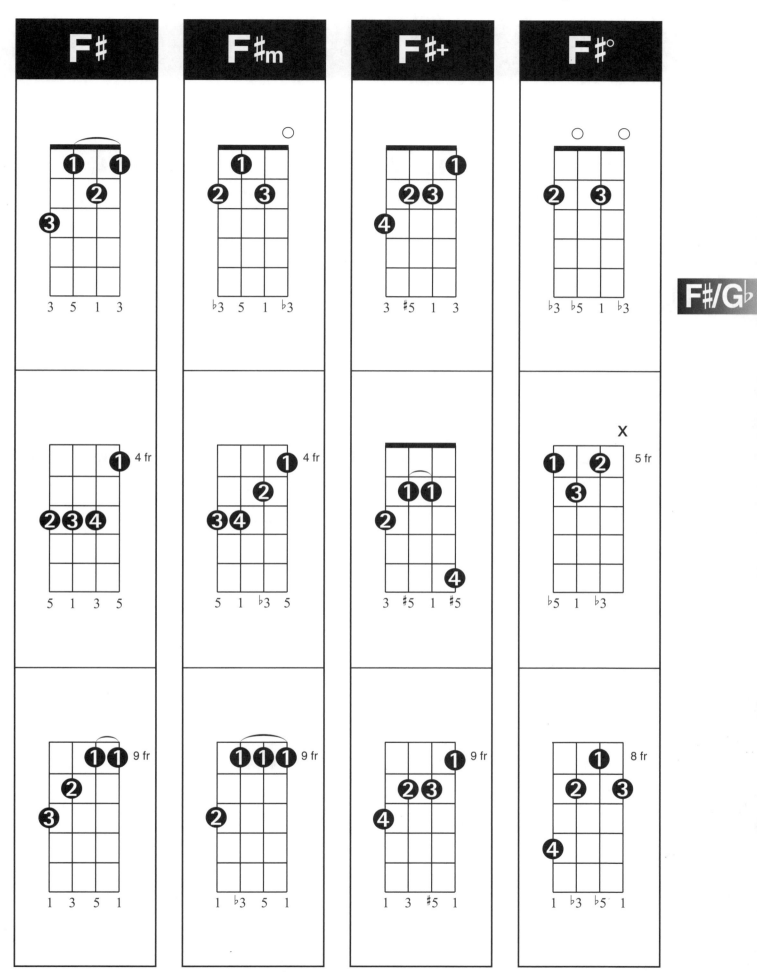

DGBE = C#/Db

F#/Gb

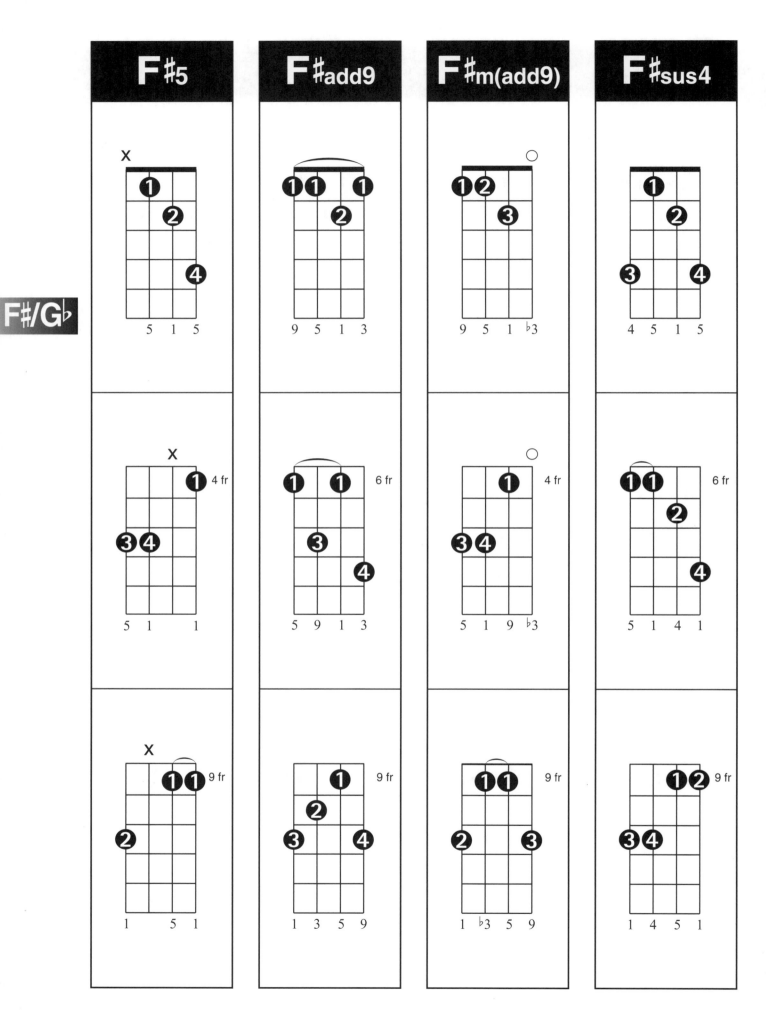

F#5 F#add9 F#m(add9) F#sus4

F#/Gb

52

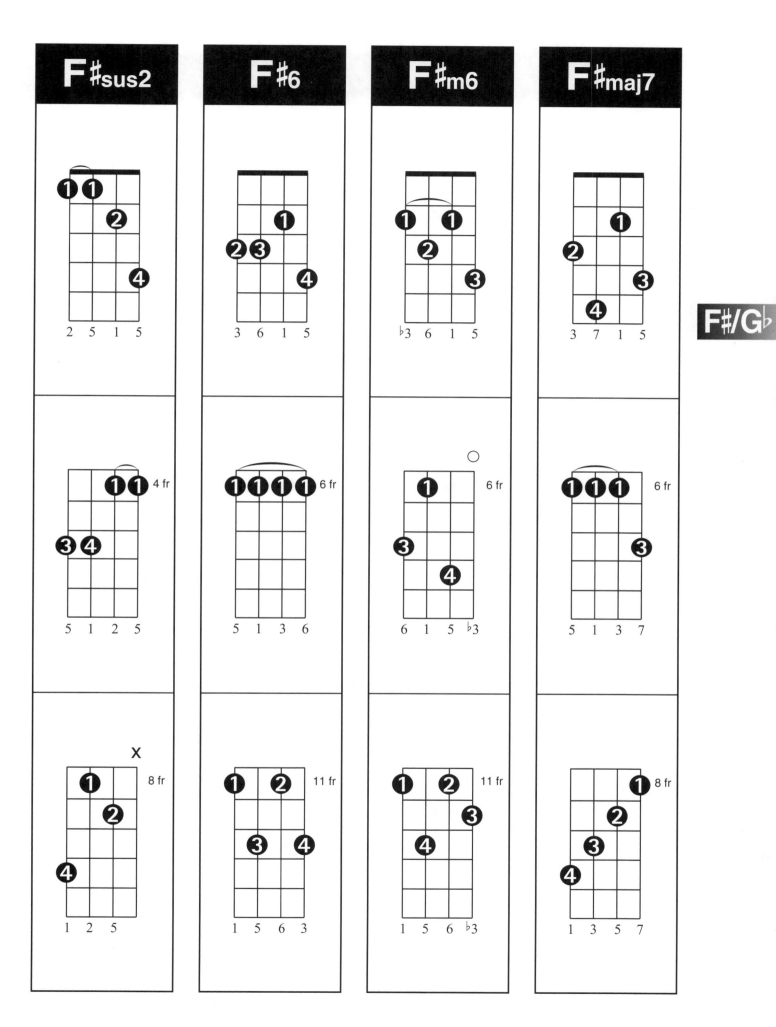

F#maj9

6 fr

7 9 3 1

9 fr

9 3 7 1

10 fr

1 3 7 9

F#m7

♭3 ♭7 1 5

6 fr

♭7 1 5 ♭3

11 fr

1 5 ♭7 ♭3

F#m(maj7)

♭3 7 1 5

6 fr

7 1 5 ♭3

11 fr

1 5 7 ♭3

F#m7♭5

♭3 ♭7 1 ♭5

6 fr

♭7 1 ♭5 ♭3

11 fr

1 ♭5 ♭7 ♭3

F#/G♭

54

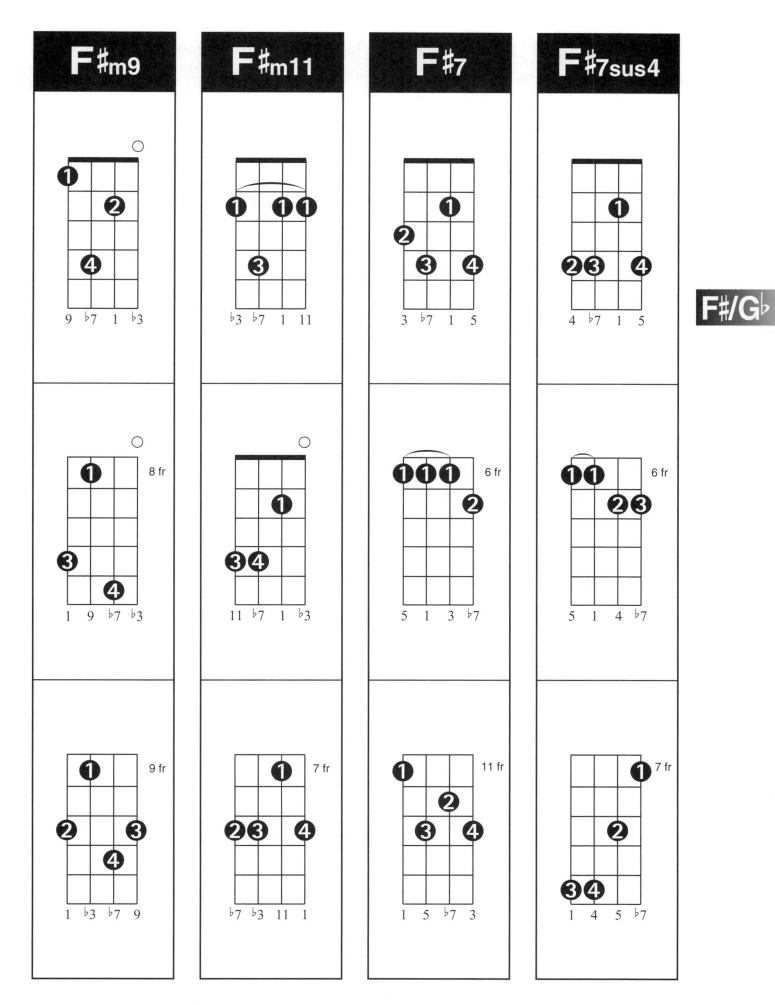

F#/Gb

F#+7

3 ♭7 1 #5

#5 1 3 ♭7 — 6 fr

♭7 3 #5 1 — 9 fr

F#7♭5

3 ♭7 1 ♭5

♭5 1 3 ♭7 — 5 fr

1 3 ♭5 ♭7 — 7 fr

F#9

9 ♭7 1 3

♭7 9 3 1 — 6 fr

1 3 ♭7 9 — 10 fr

F#7#9

3 ♭7 1 #9

♭7 3 5 #9 — 9 fr

1 3 ♭7 #9 — 10 fr

F#/G♭

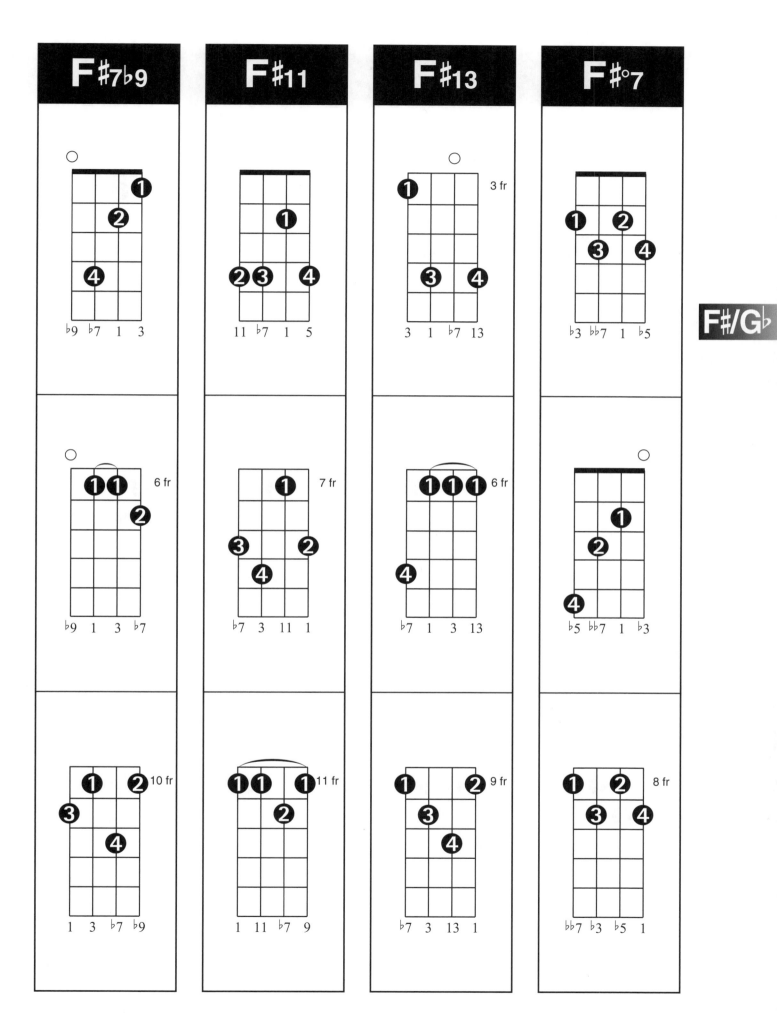

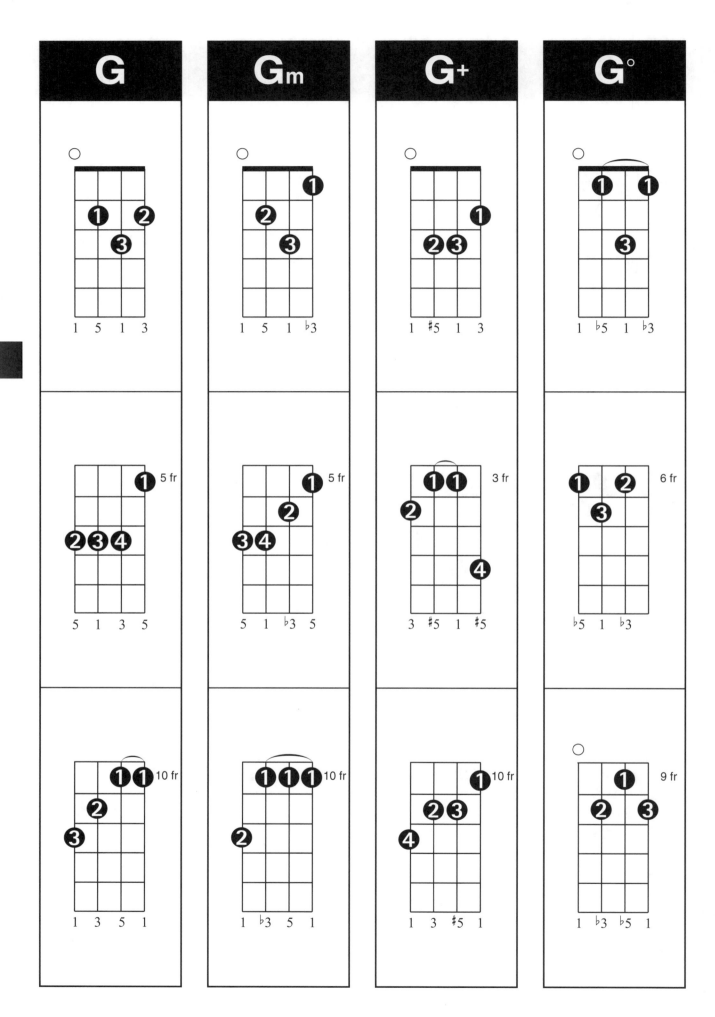

DGBE = D

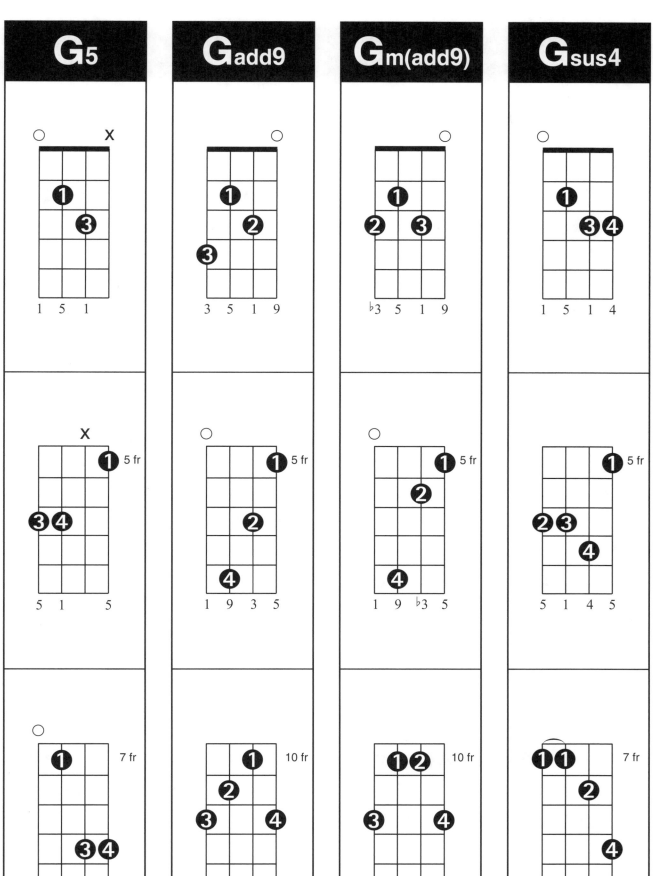

G5   Gadd9   Gm(add9)   Gsus4

G

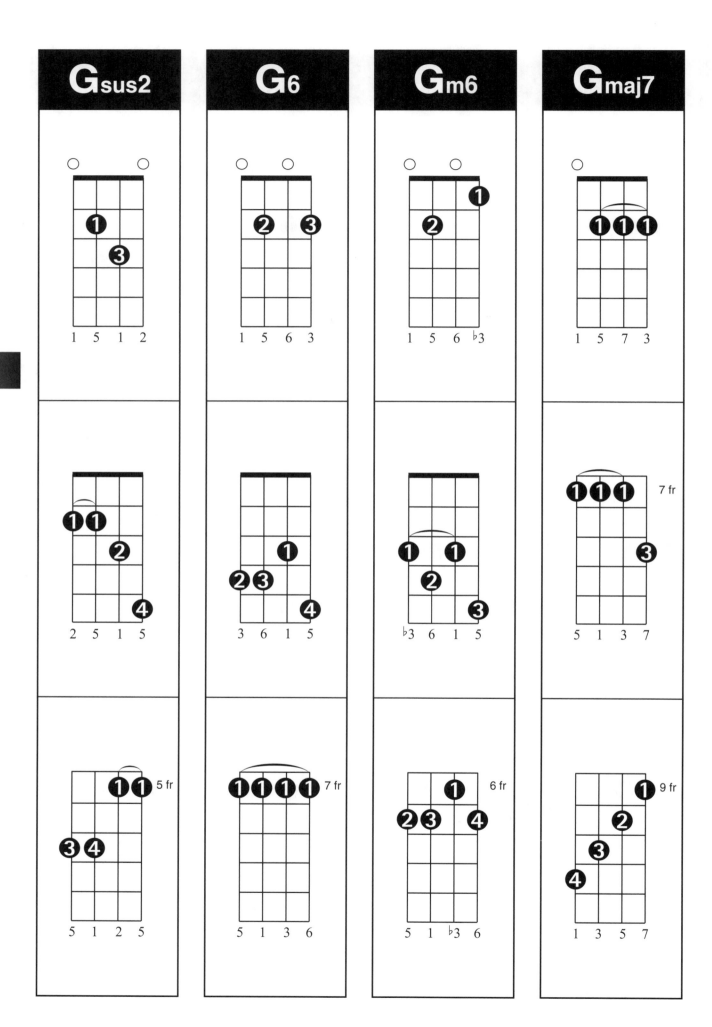

G

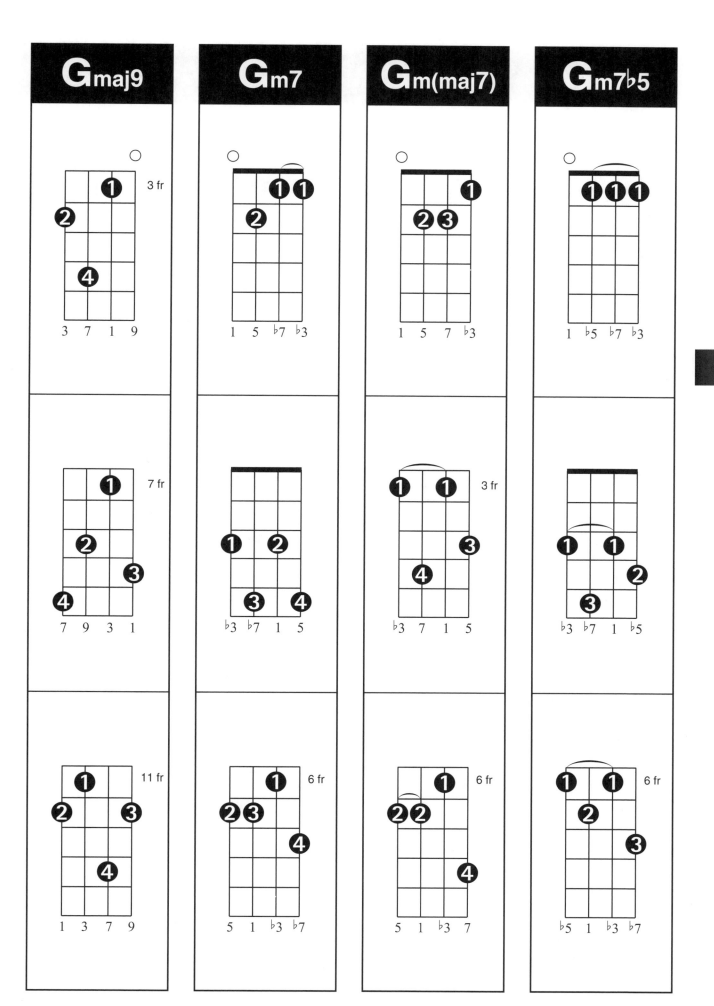

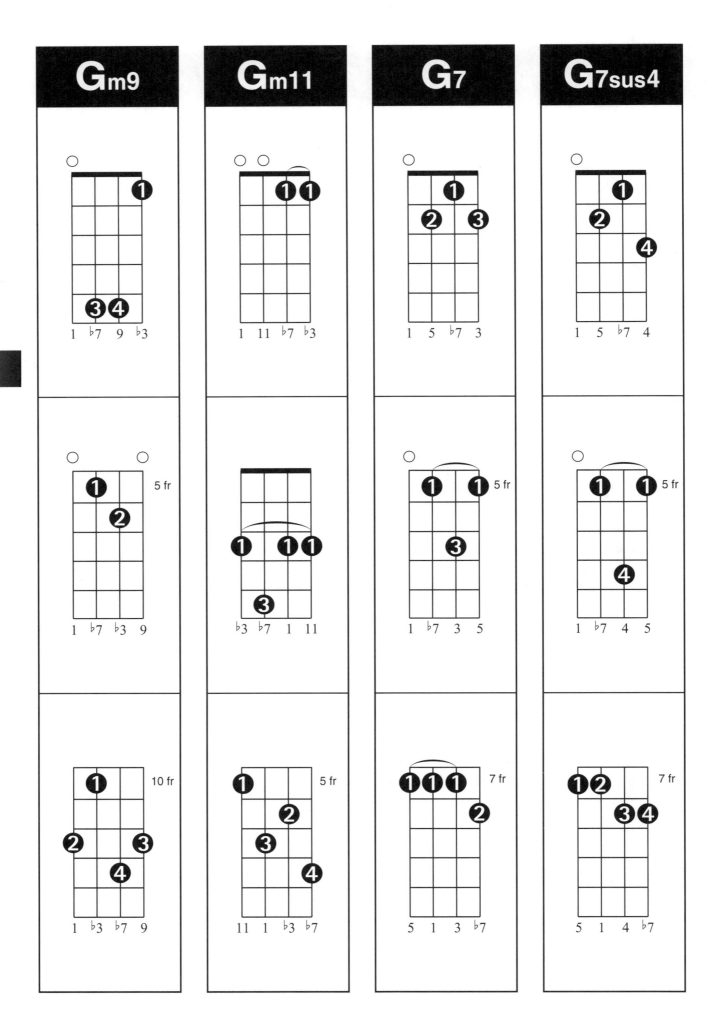

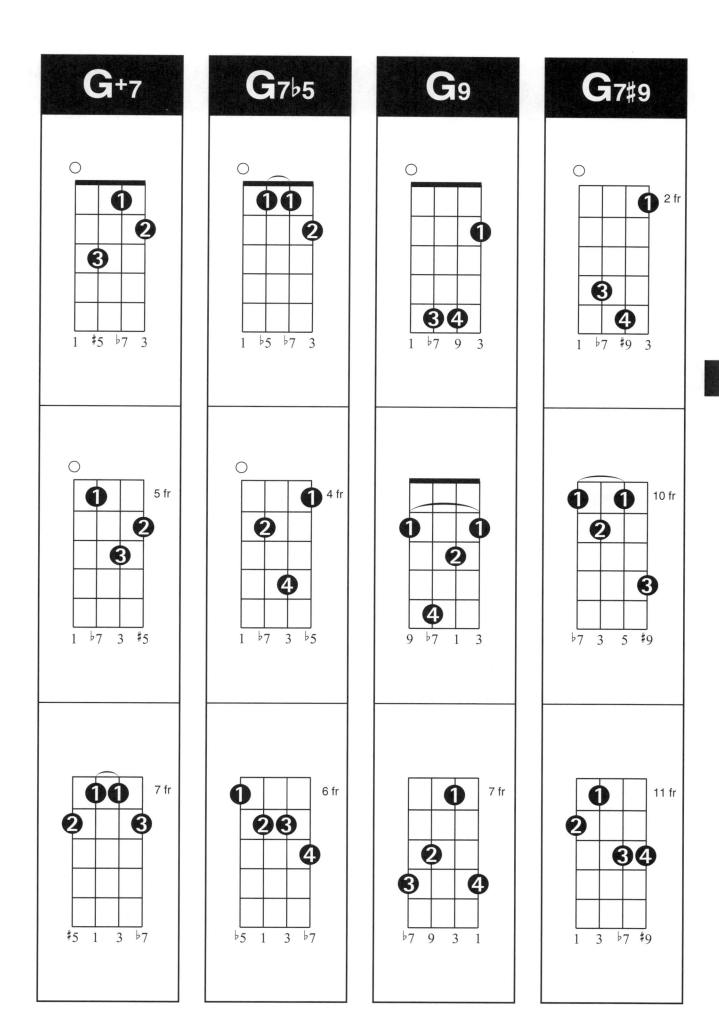

G

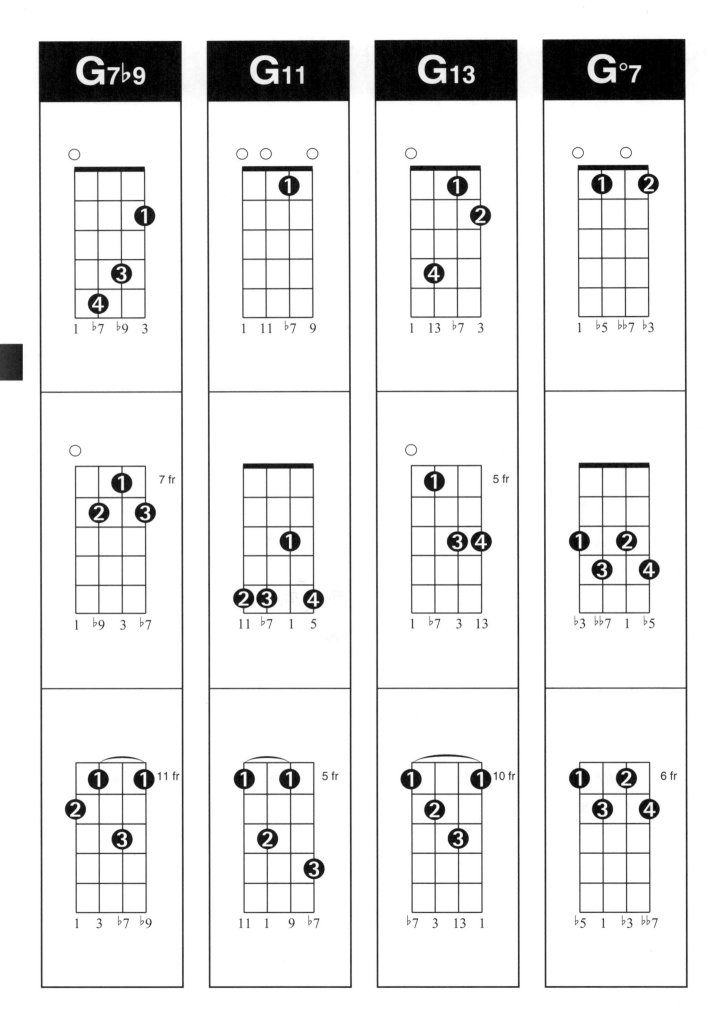

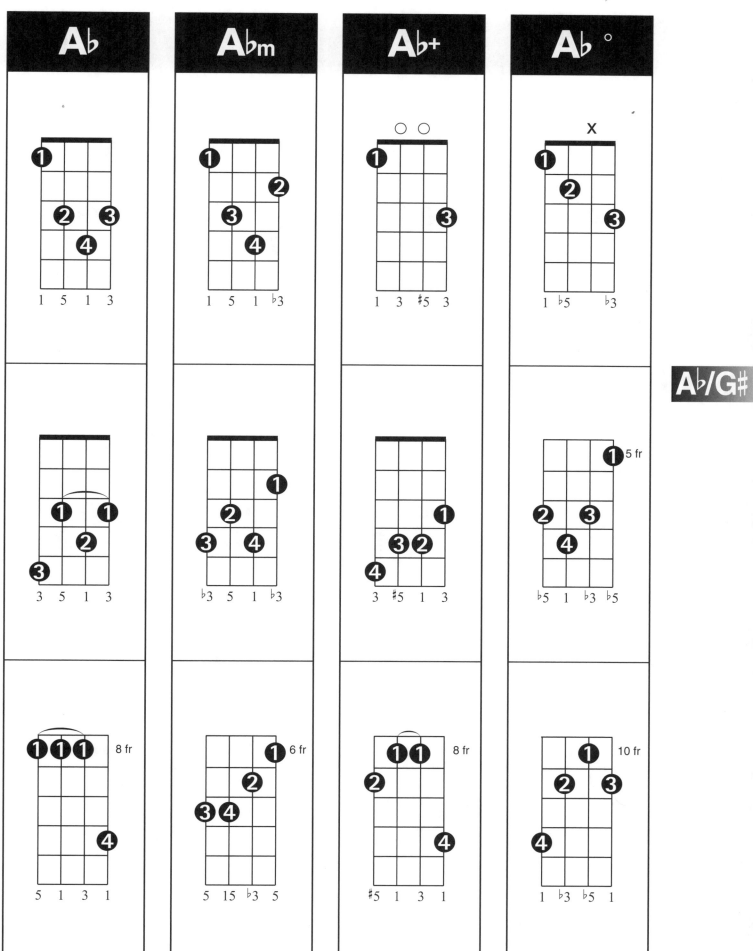

Ab   Abm   Ab+   Ab °

Ab/G#

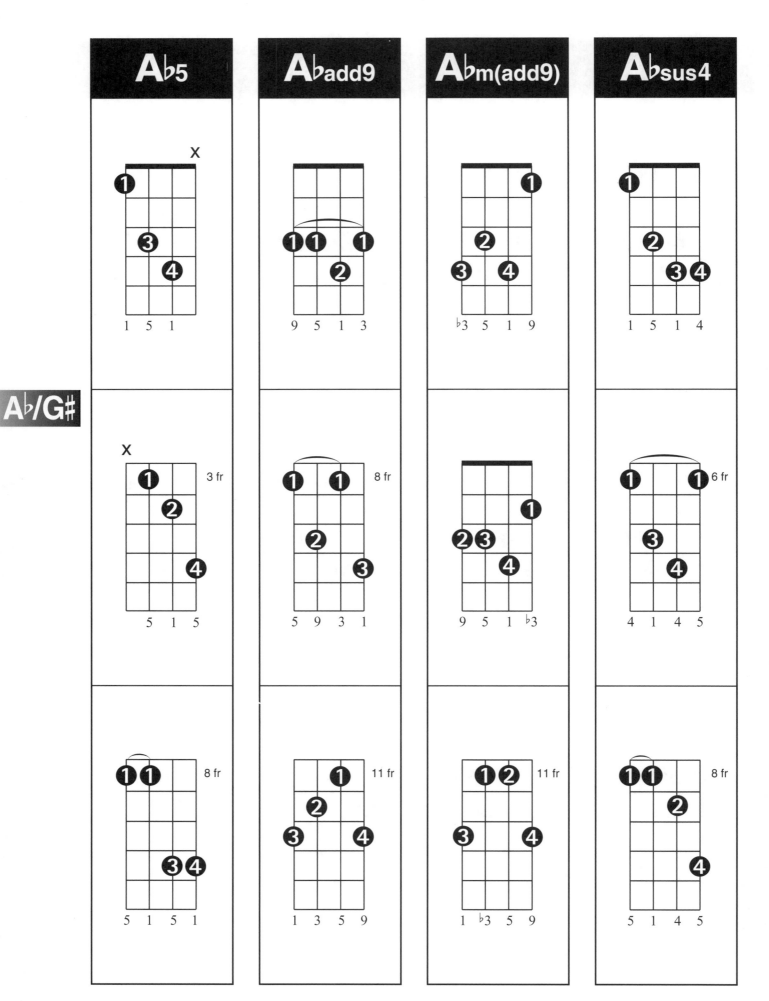

A♭sus2

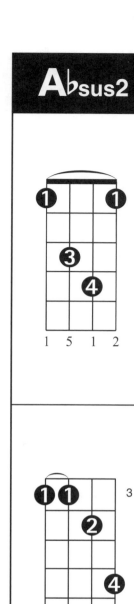

1 5 1 2

2 5 1 5

5 1 2 5

A♭6

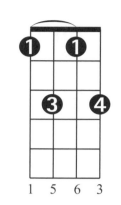

1 5 6 3

3 6 1 5

5 1 3 6

A♭m6

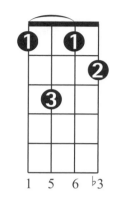

1 5 6 ♭3

♭3 6 1 5

5 1 ♭3 6

A♭maj7

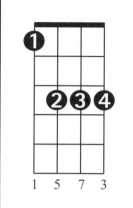

1 5 7 3

3 7 1 5

5 1 3 7

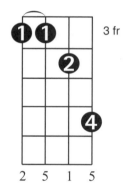
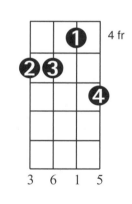
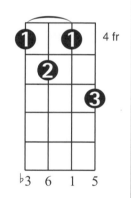
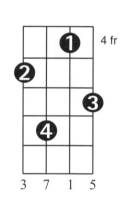
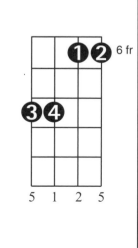
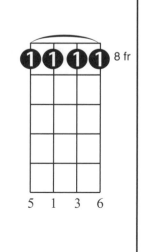
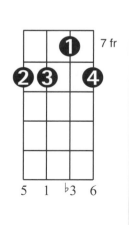
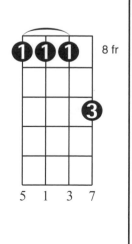

A♭/G#

| A♭maj9 | A♭m7 | A♭m(maj7) | A♭m7♭5 |

A♭/G#

68

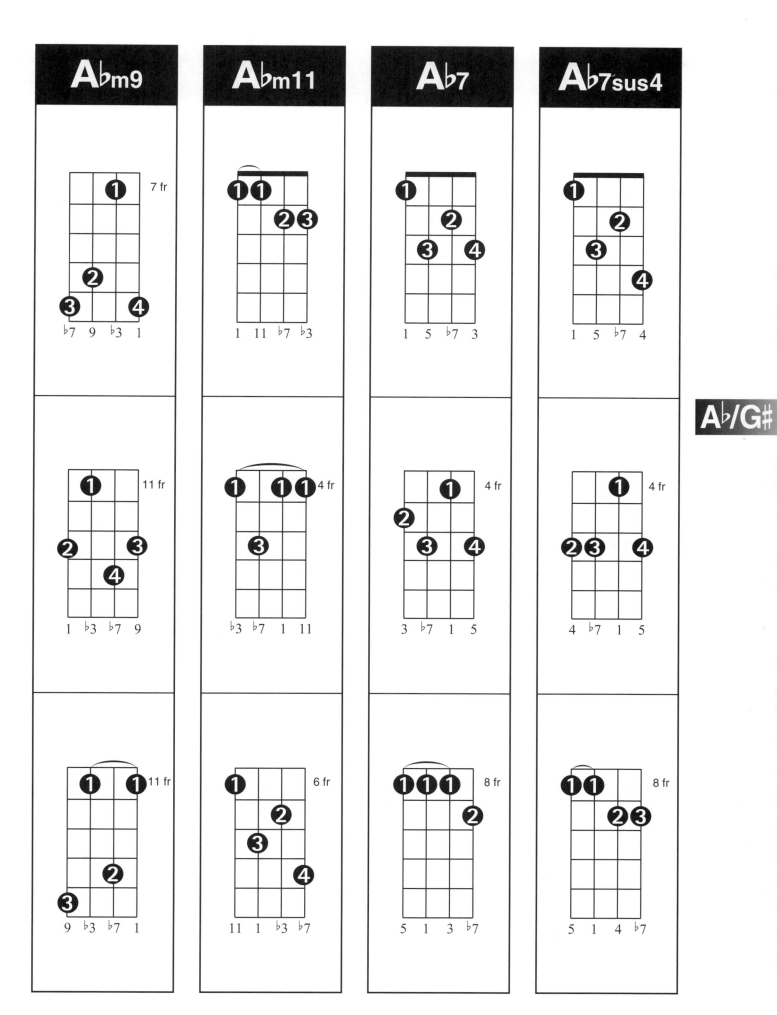

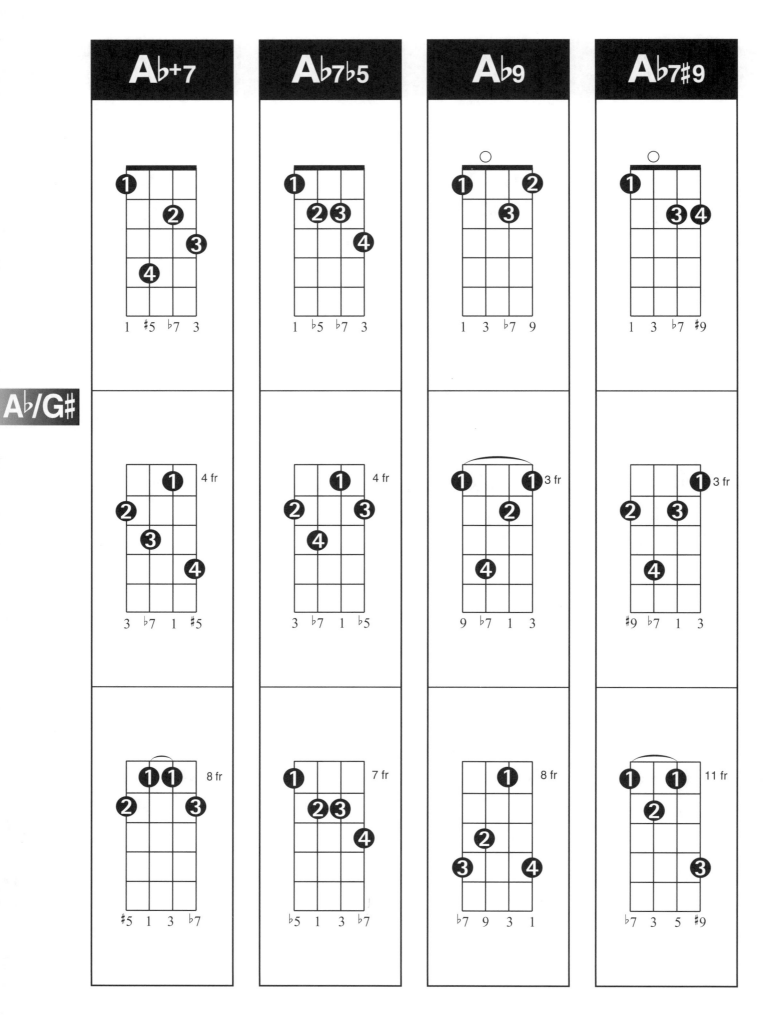

A♭7♭9

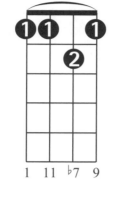

1 3 ♭7 ♭9

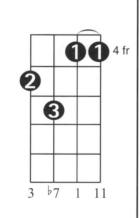

4 fr

3 ♭7 1 ♭9

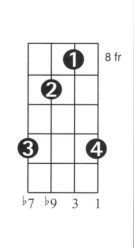

8 fr

♭7 ♭9 3 1

A♭11

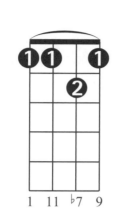

1 11 ♭7 9

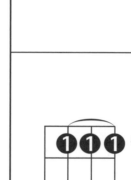

4 fr

3 ♭7 1 11

6 fr

11 1 3 ♭7

A♭13

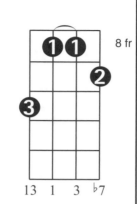

8 fr

13 1 3 ♭7

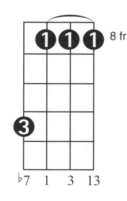

8 fr

♭7 1 3 13

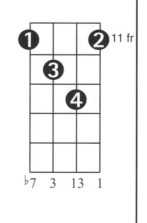

11 fr

♭7 3 13 1

A♭°7

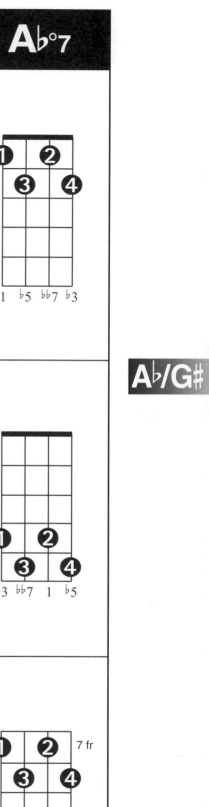

1 ♭5 ♭♭7 ♭3

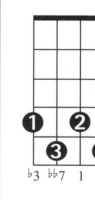

♭3 ♭♭7 1 ♭5

7 fr

♭5 1 ♭3 ♭♭7

A♭/G#

71

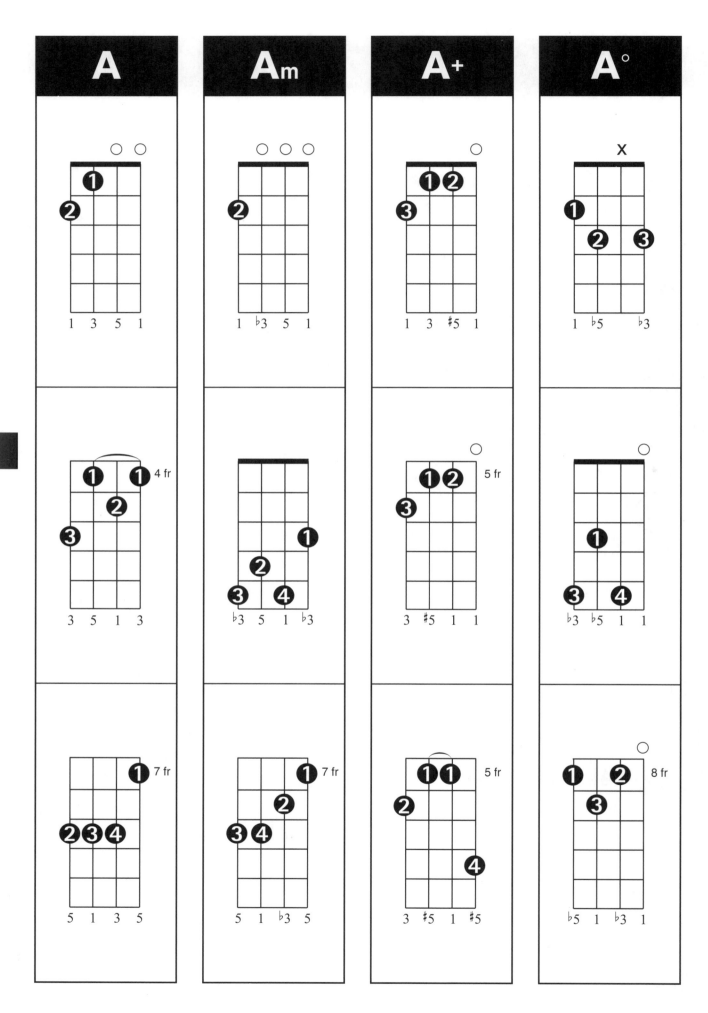

DGBE =E

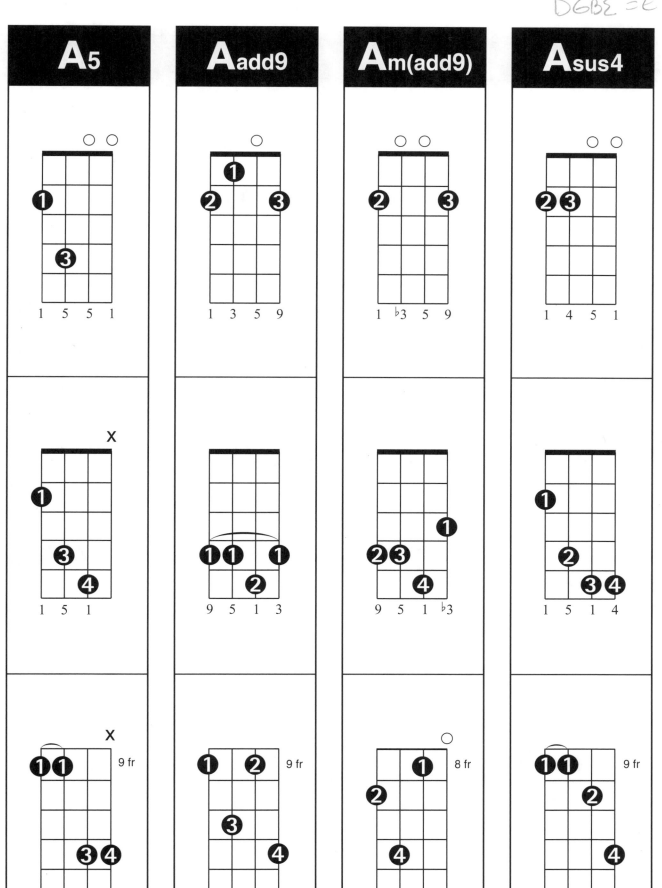

A5   Aadd9   Am(add9)   Asus4

Asus2

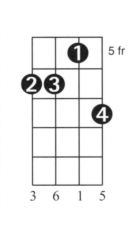

1 5 2

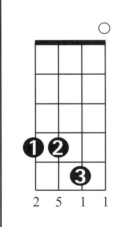

2 5 1 1

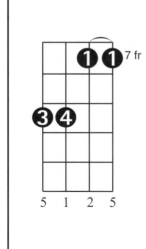

7 fr

5 1 2 5

A6

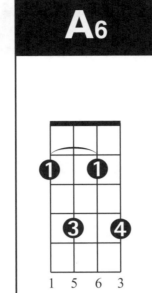

1 5 6 3

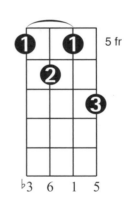

5 fr

3 6 1 5

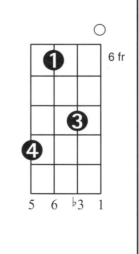

6 fr

5 6 3 1

Am6

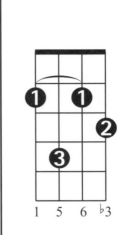

1 5 6 ♭3

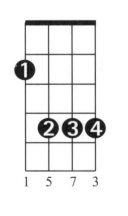

5 fr

♭3 6 1 5

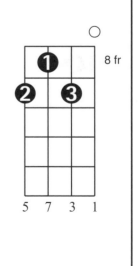

6 fr

5 6 ♭3 1

Amaj7

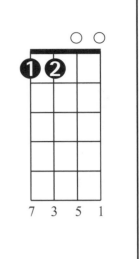

7 3 5 1

1 5 7 3

8 fr

5 7 3 1

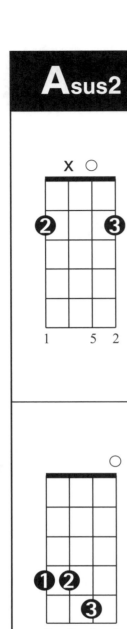

A

74

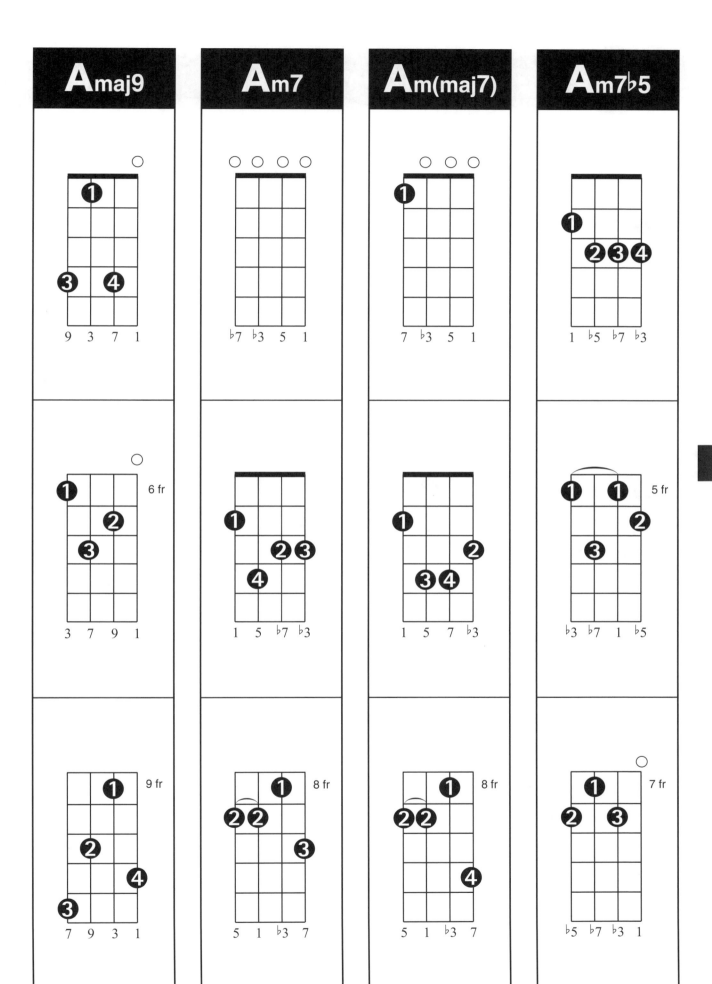

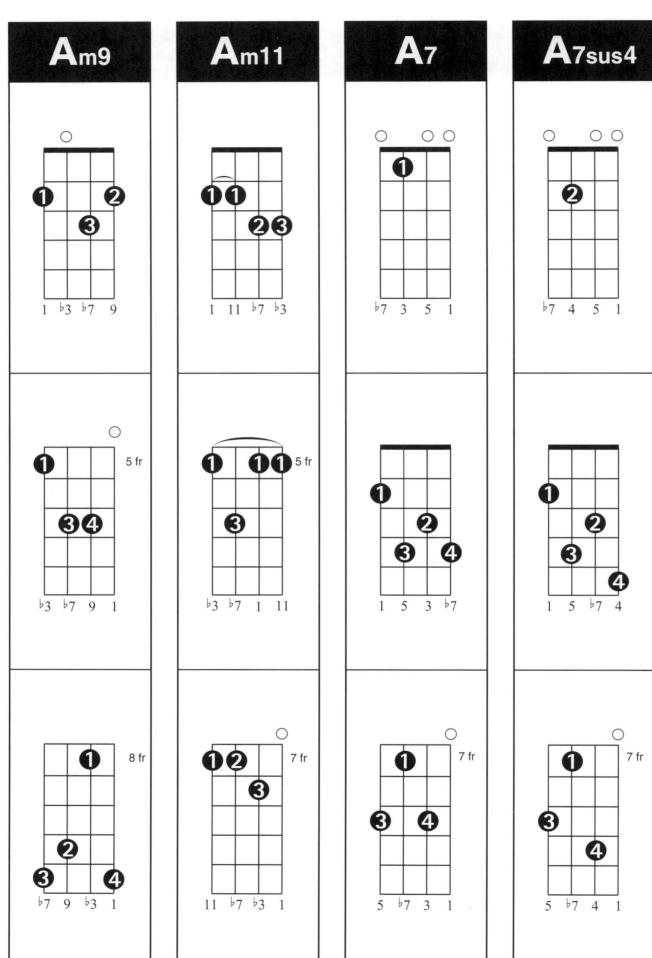

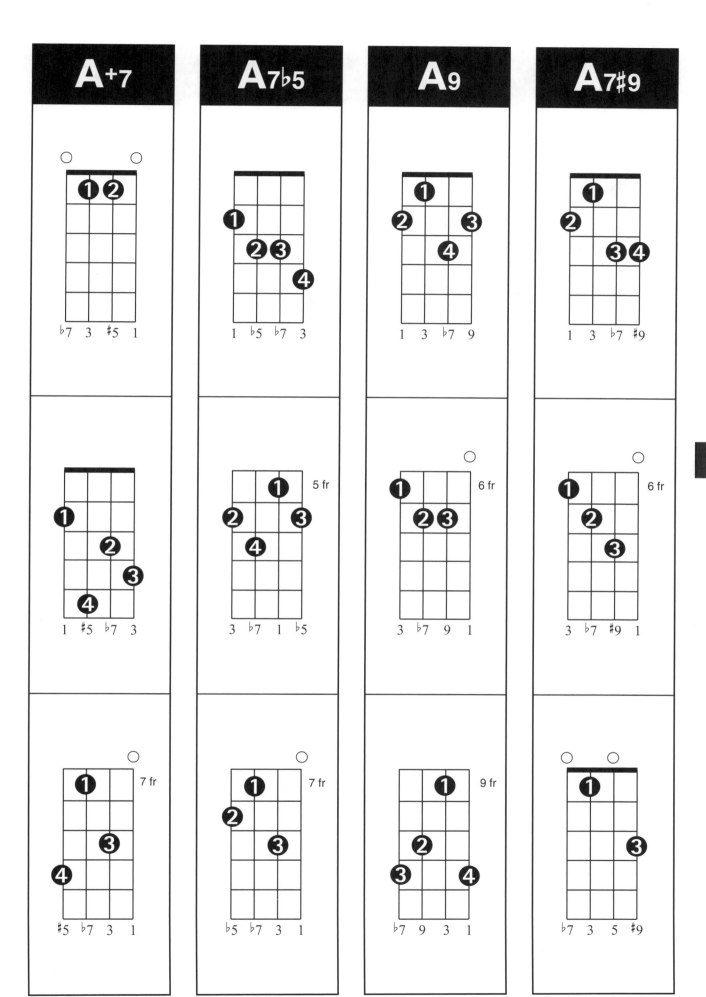

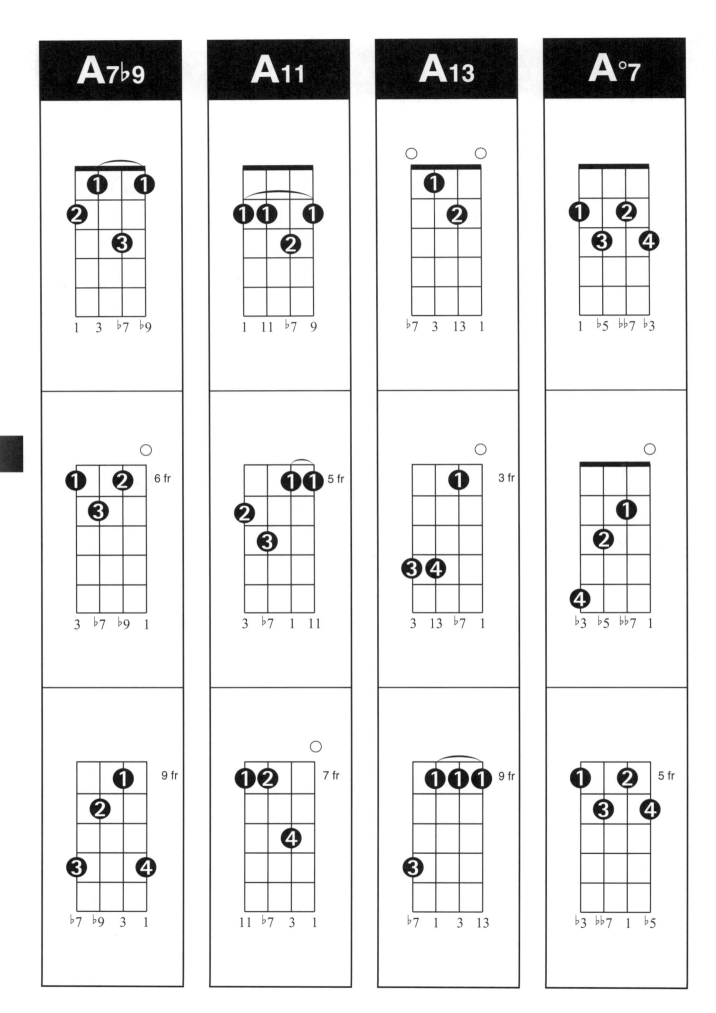

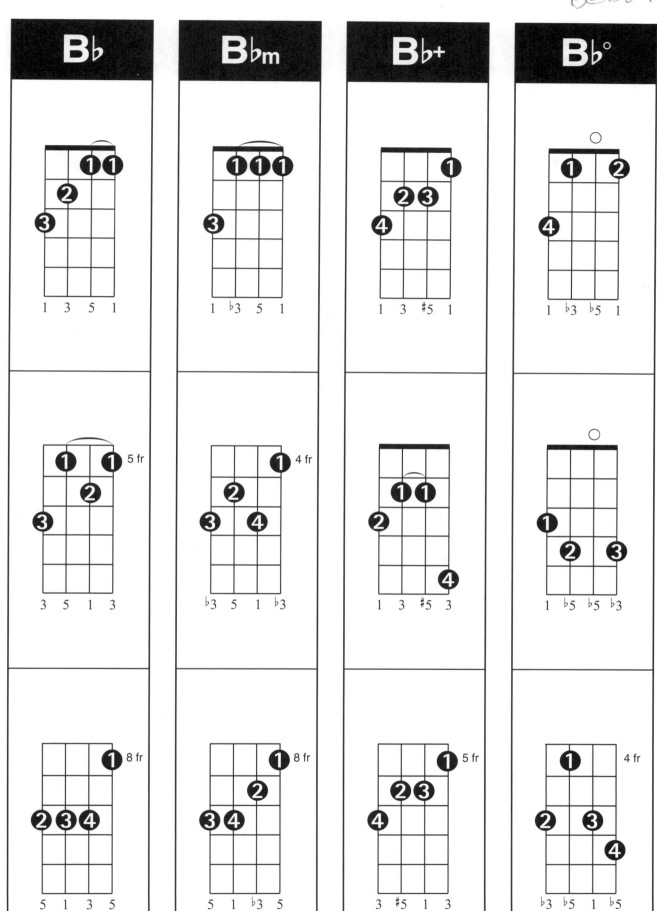

B♭/A#

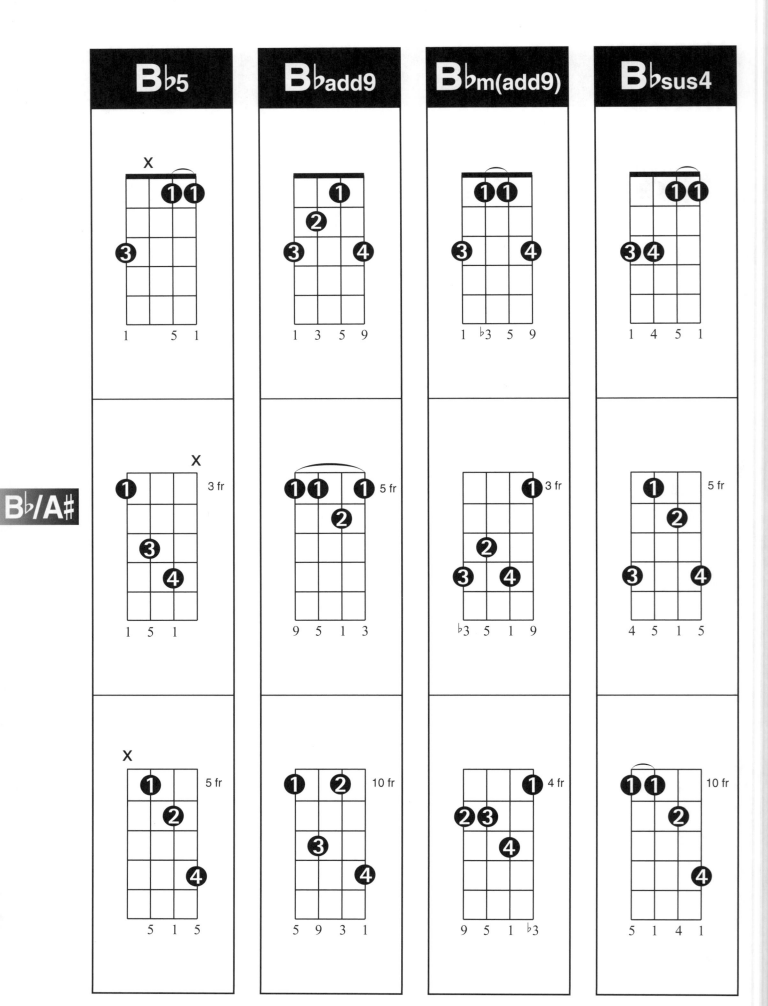

Bb5   Bbadd9   Bbm(add9)   Bbsus4

Bb/A#

80

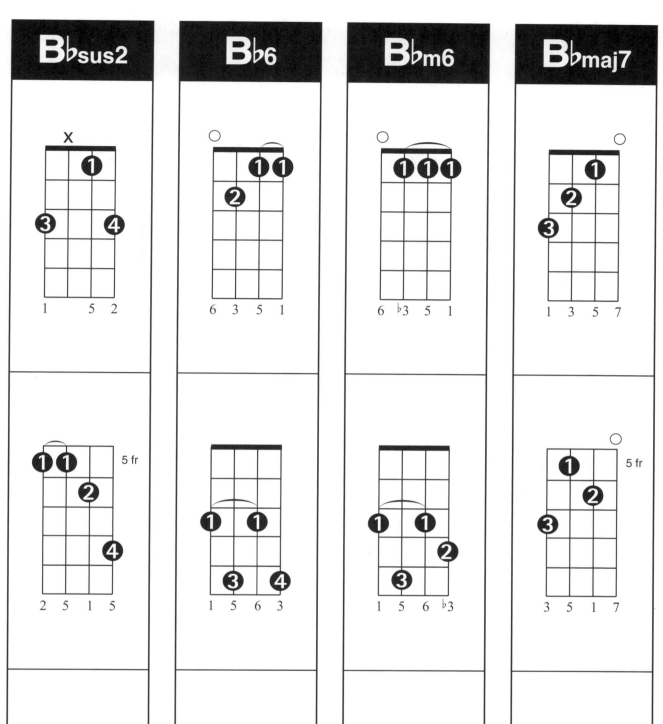

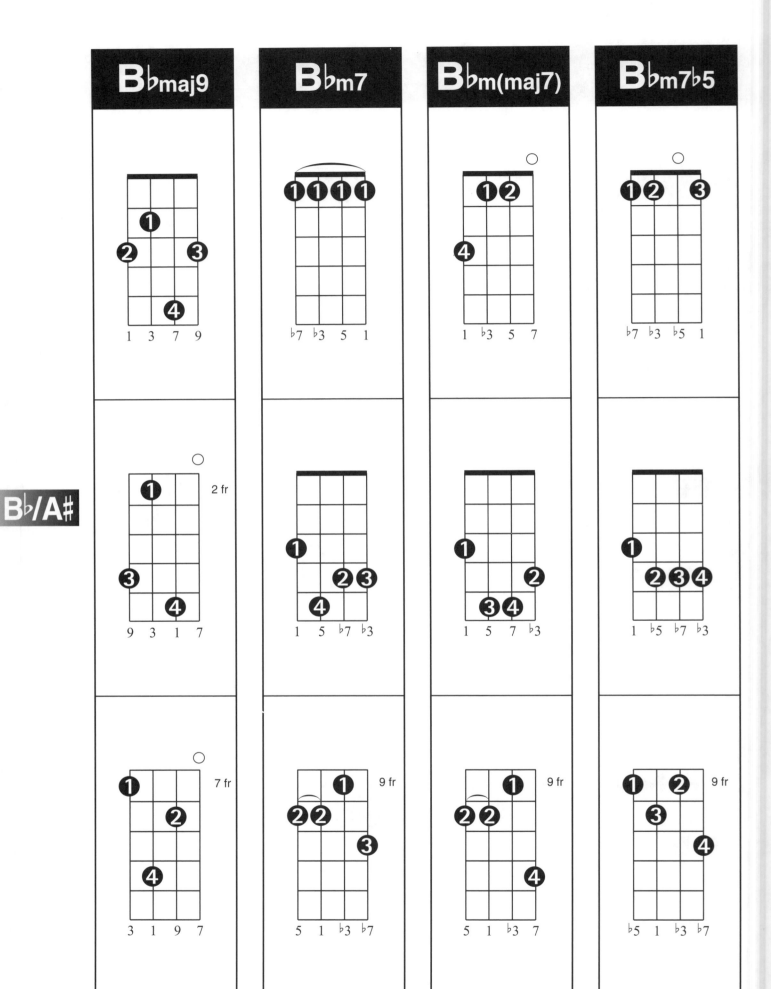

B♭maj9   B♭m7   B♭m(maj7)   B♭m7♭5

B♭/A#

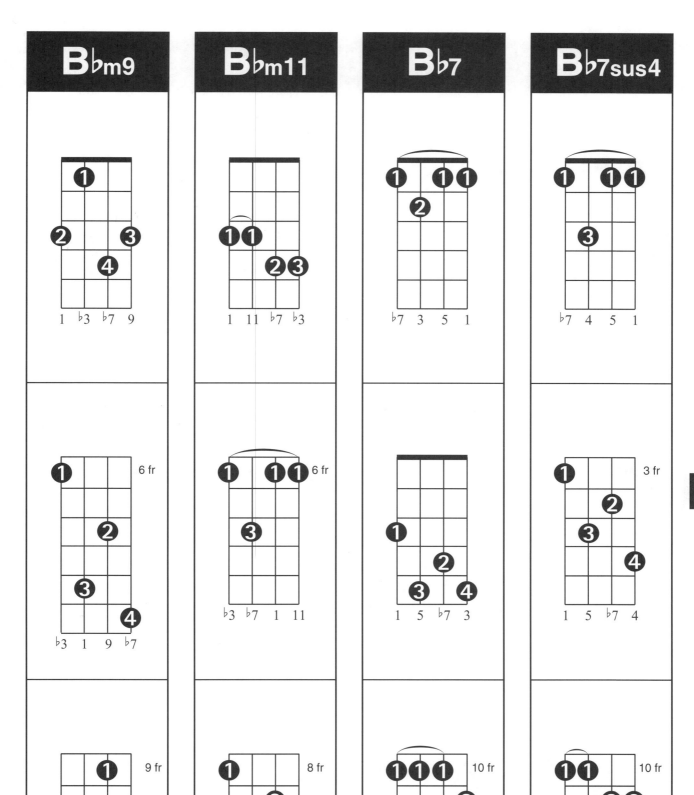

B♭m9 B♭m11 B♭7 B♭7sus4

B♭/A#

83

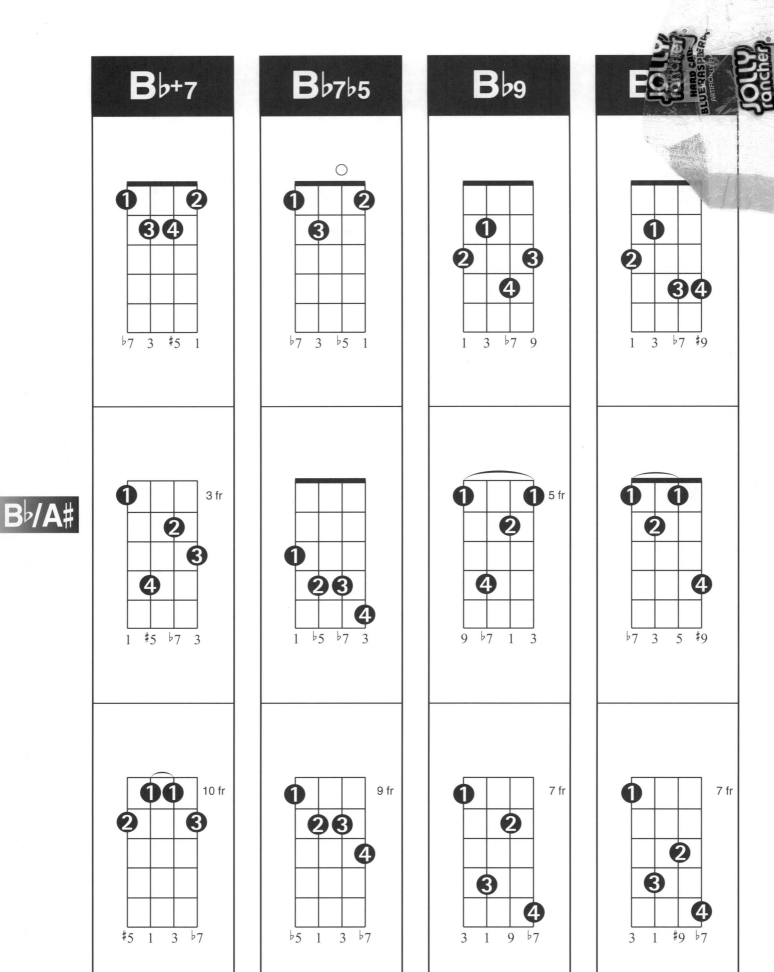

Bb7b9   Bb11   Bb13   Bb°7

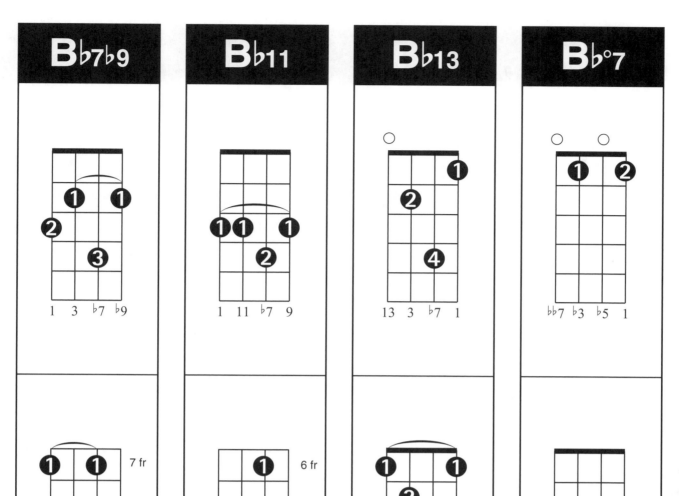

Bb7b9 — 1 3 ♭7 ♭9

Bb11 — 1 11 ♭7 9

Bb13 — 13 3 ♭7 1

Bb°7 — ♭♭7 ♭3 ♭5 1

Bb/A#

Bb7b9 (7 fr) — 3 1 ♭9 ♭7

Bb11 (6 fr) — 11 ♭7 1 5

Bb13 (6 fr) — ♭7 3 13 1

Bb°7 — 1 ♭5 ♭♭7 ♭3

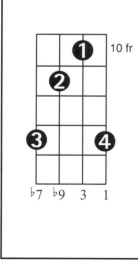

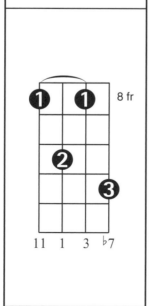

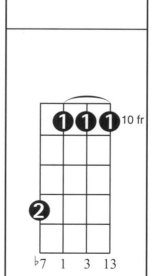

Bb7b9 (10 fr) — ♭7 ♭9 3 1

Bb11 (8 fr) — 11 1 3 ♭7

Bb13 (10 fr) — ♭7 1 3 13

Bb°7 (6 fr) — ♭3 ♭♭7 1 ♭5

B

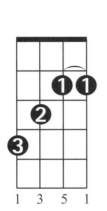

1 3 5 1

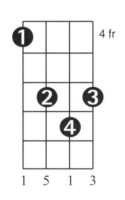

4 fr

1 5 1 3

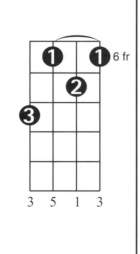

6 fr

3 5 1 3

Bm

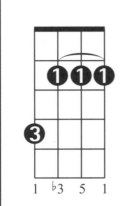

1 ♭3 5 1

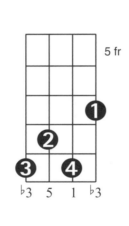

5 fr

♭3 5 1 ♭3

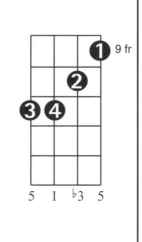

9 fr

5 1 ♭3 5

B+

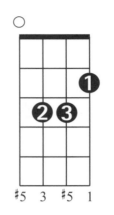

#5 3 #5 1

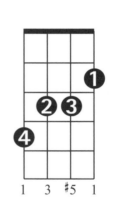

1 3 #5 1

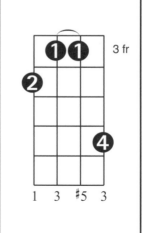

3 fr

1 3 #5 3

B°

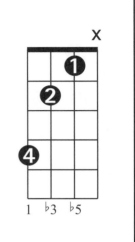

1 ♭3 ♭5

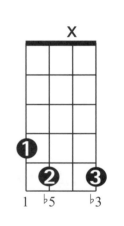

1 ♭5 ♭3

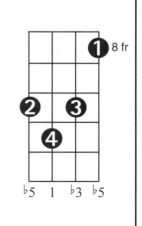

8 fr

♭5 1 ♭3 ♭5

B

B5

Badd9

Bm(add9)

Bsus4

B

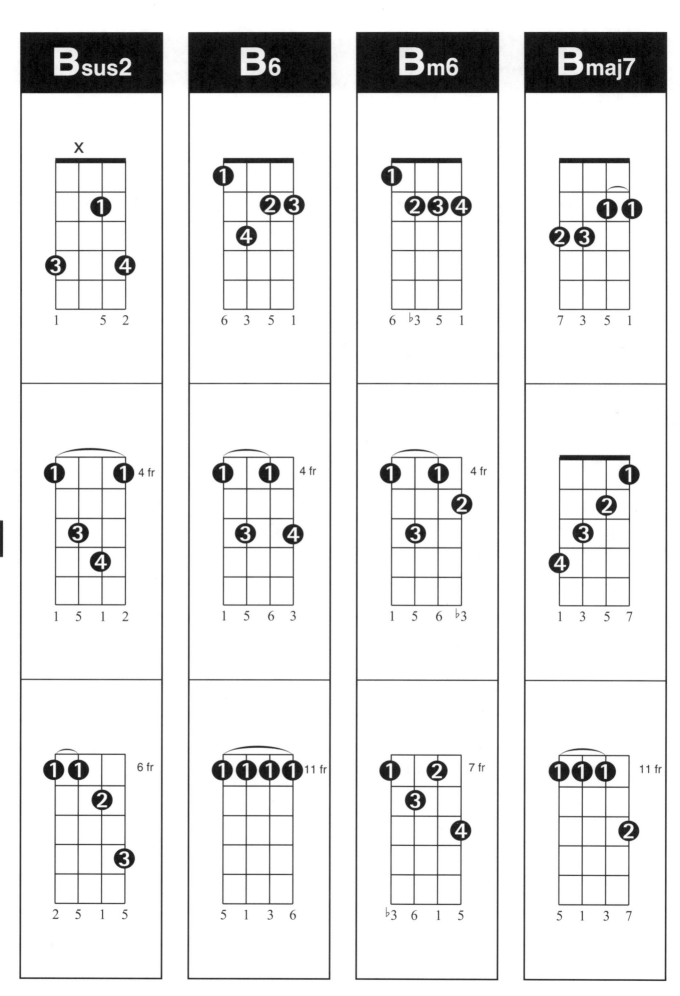

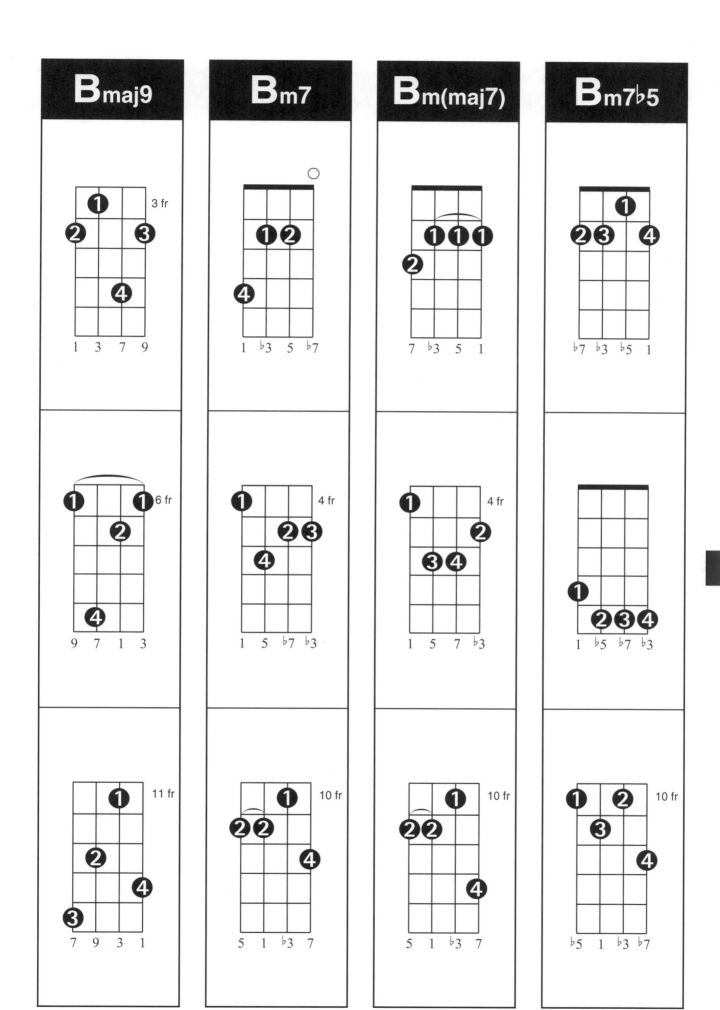

Bm9

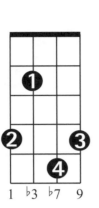

1 ♭3 ♭7 9

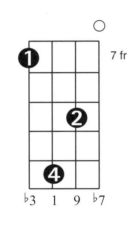
7 fr

♭3 1 9 ♭7

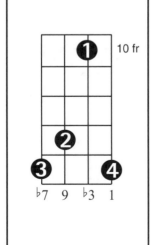
10 fr

♭7 9 ♭3 1

Bm11

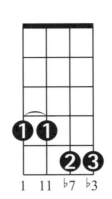

1 11 ♭7 ♭3

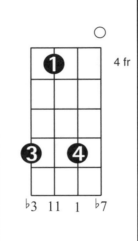
4 fr

♭3 11 1 ♭7

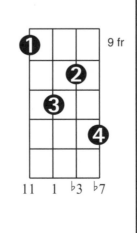
9 fr

11 1 ♭3 ♭7

B7

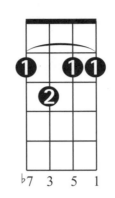

♭7 3 5 1

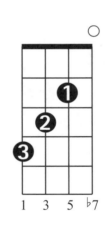

1 3 5 ♭7

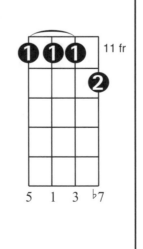
11 fr

5 1 3 ♭7

B7sus4

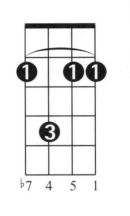

♭7 4 5 1

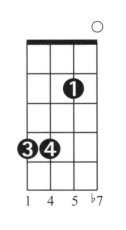

1 4 5 ♭7

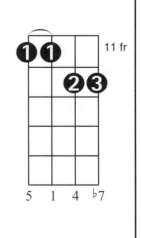
11 fr

5 1 4 ♭7

B

Learn To Play Today
with folk music instruction from

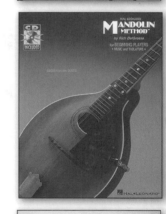

Prices and availability subject to change without notice.